CliffsNotes™

Swift's
Gulliver's Travels

By A. Lewis Soens, Jr., Ph.D. and Patrick Salerno

IN THIS BOOK

- Learn about the Life and Background of the Author
- Preview an Introduction to the Novel
- Study a graphical Character Map
- Explore themes and literary devices in the Critical Commentaries
- Examine in-depth Character Analyses
- Enhance your understanding of the work with Critical Essays
- Reinforce what you learn with CliffsNotes Review
- Find additional information to further your study in CliffsNotes Resource Center and online at www.cliffsnotes.com

IDG BOOKS
WORLDWIDE

IDG Books Worldwide, Inc.
An International Data Group Company
Foster City, CA • Chicago, IL • Indianapolis, IN • New York, NY

About the Author

A. Lewis Soens, Jr., received his Ph.D. in English from Princeton University and has taught in several distinguished departments of English, including at the University of Colorado and the University of Notre Dame.

Patrick Salerno has worked as a teacher of language, literature, and composition, and as a curriculum developer in the fields of English and language arts.

Publisher's Acknowledgments

Editorial

Project Editor: Tracy Barr

Acquisitions Editor: Greg Tubach

Glossary Editors: The editors and staff at Webster's New World Dictionaries

Editorial Administrator: Michelle Hacker

Production

Indexer: York Production Services, Inc.

Proofreader: York Production Services, Inc.

IDG Books Indianapolis Production Department

CliffsNotes™ Swift's *Gulliver's Travels*

Published by

IDG Books Worldwide, Inc.

An International Data Group Company

919 E. Hillsdale Blvd.

Suite 300

Foster City, CA 94404

www.idgbooks.com (IDG Books Worldwide Web site)

www.cliffsnotes.com (CliffsNotes Web site)

Library of Congress Control Number: 00-107688

ISBN: 0-7645-8678-5

Printed in the United States of America

10 9 8 7 6 5 4 3 2 1

1O/RU/RR/QQ/IN

Distributed in the United States by IDG Books Worldwide, Inc.

Distributed by CDG Books Canada Inc. for Canada; by Transworld Publishers Limited in the United Kingdom; by IDG Norge Books for Norway; by IDG Sweden Books for Sweden; by IDG Books Australia Publishing Corporation Pty. Ltd. for Australia and New Zealand; by TransQuest Publishers Pte Ltd. for Singapore, Malaysia, Thailand, Indonesia, and Hong Kong; by Gotop Information Inc. for Taiwan; by ICG Muse, Inc. for Japan; by Intersoft for South Africa; by Eyrolles for France; by International Thomson Publishing for Germany, Austria and Switzerland; by Distribuidora Cuspide for Argentina; by LR International for Brazil; by Galileo Libros for Chile; by Ediciones ZETA S.C.R. Ltda. for Peru; by WS Computer Publishing Corporation, Inc., for the Philippines; by Contemporanea de Ediciones for Venezuela; by Express Computer Distributors for the Caribbean and West Indies; by Micronesia Media Distributor, Inc. for Micronesia; by Chips Computadoras S.A. de C.V. for Mexico; by Editorial Norma de Panama S.A. for Panama; by American Bookshops for Finland.

For general information on IDG Books Worldwide's books in the U.S., please call our Consumer Customer Service department at **800-762-2974.** For reseller information, including discounts and premium sales, please call our Reseller Customer Service department at **800-434-3422.**

For information on where to purchase IDG Books Worldwide's books outside the U.S., please contact our International Sales department at **317-596-5530** or fax **317-572-4002.**

For consumer information on foreign language translations, please contact our Customer Service department at **1-800-434-3422**, fax **317-572-4002**, or e-mail rights@idgbooks.com.

For information on licensing foreign or domestic rights, please phone **+1-650-653-7098.**

For sales inquiries and special prices for bulk quantities, please contact our Order Services department at **800-434-3422** or write to the address above.

For information on using IDG Books Worldwide's books in the classroom or for ordering examination copies, please contact our Educational Sales department at **800-434-2086** or fax **317-572-4005.**

For press review copies, author interviews, or other publicity information, please contact our Public Relations department at **650-653-7000** or fax **650-653-7500.**

For authorization to photocopy items for corporate, personal, or educational use, please contact Copyright Clearance Center, 222 Rosewood Drive, Danvers, MA 01923, or fax **978-750-4470.**

is a registered trademark under exclusive license to IDG Books Worldwide, Inc. from International Data Group, Inc.

Table of Contents

Life and Background of the Author 1

Early Years and Education 2

Career 2

Major Literary Works 3

Introduction to the Novel 4

Introduction 5

A Brief Synopsis 5

List of Characters 7

Character Map 9

Critical Commentaries 10

Book I: A Voyage to Lilliput 11

Chapter 1 11

Summary 11

Commentary 11

Glossary 12

Chapter 2 13

Summary 13

Commentary 13

Glossary 14

Chapter 3 15

Summary 15

Commentary 15

Glossary 16

Chapter 4 17

Summary 17

Commentary 17

Glossary 18

Chapter 5 19

Summary 19

Commentary 19

Glossary 20

Chapter 6 21

Summary 21

Commentary 21

Glossary 22

Chapter 7 23

Summary 23

Commentary 23

Glossary 24

Chapter 8 25
    Summary 25
    Commentary 25
    Glossary 26
Book II: A Voyage to Brobdingnag 27
Chapter 1 27
    Summary 27
    Commentary 27
    Glossary 28
Chapter 2 29
    Summary 29
    Commentary 29
    Glossary 30
Chapter 3 31
    Summary 31
    Commentary 31
    Glossary 32
Chapter 4 33
    Summary 33
    Commentary 33
    Glossary 33
Chapter 5 34
    Summary 34
    Commentary 34
    Glossary 35
Chapter 6 36
    Summary 36
    Commentary 36
    Glossary 37
Chapter 7 38
    Summary 38
    Commentary 38
    Glossary 39
Chapter 8 40
    Summary 40
    Commentary 40
    Glossary 40
Book III: A Voyage to Laputa, Balnibarbi, Luggnagg,
Glubbdubdrib, and Japan 41
Chapter 1 41
    Summary 41
    Commentary 41
    Glossary 42

Chapter 2 43
   Summary 43
   Commentary 43
   Glossary 44
Chapter 3 45
   Summary 45
   Commentary 45
   Glossary 46
Chapter 4 47
   Summary 47
   Commentary 47
Chapter 5 48
   Summary 48
   Commentary 48
   Glossary 48
Chapter 6 49
   Summary 49
   Commentary 49
   Glossary 49
Chapter 7 50
   Summary 50
   Commentary 50
   Glossary 50
Chapter 8 51
   Summary 51
   Commentary 51
   Glossary 52
Chapter 9 53
   Summary 53
   Commentary 53
   Glossary 53
Chapter 10 54
   Summary 54
   Commentary 54
Chapter 11 55
   Summary 55
   Commentary 55
   Glossary 55
Book IV: A Voyage to the Country of the Houyhnhnms 56
Chapter 1 56
   Summary 56

Commentary 56
Glossary 57
Chapter 2 58
Summary 58
Commentary 58
Glossary 59
Chapter 3 60
Summary 60
Commentary 60
Glossary 61
Chapter 4 62
Summary 62
Commentary 62
Glossary 63
Chapter 5 64
Summary 64
Commentary 64
Glossary 64
Chapter 6 65
Summary 65
Commentary 65
Glossary 66
Chapter 7 67
Summary 67
Commentary 67
Glossary 67
Chapter 8 68
Summary 68
Commentary 68
Glossary 68
Chapter 9 69
Summary 69
Commentary 69
Glossary 70
Chapter 10 71
Summary 71
Commentary 71
Glossary 72

Chapter 11 73
    Summary 73
    Commentary 73
    Glossary 74
Chapter 12 75
    Summary 75
    Commentary 75
    Glossary 75

Character Analysis **76**
    Lemuel Gulliver 77
    The Lilliputians 78
    The Brobdingnagians 79
    The Houyhnhnms 80
    The Yahoos 81

Critical Essays **82**
    Philosophical and Political Background 83
    Swift's Satire 88
    Gulliver as a Dramatis Persona 90

CliffsNotes Review **93**
    Q&A 93

CliffsNotes Resource Center **96**
    Films and Other Recordings 97
    Magazines and Journals 98

Index **99**

How to Use This Book

CliffsNotes Swift's *Gulliver's Travels* supplements the original work, giving you background information about the author, an introduction to the novel, a graphical character map, critical commentaries, expanded glossaries, and a comprehensive index. CliffsNotes Review tests your comprehension of the original text and reinforces learning with questions and answers, practice projects, and more. For further information on Morrison and *Gulliver's Travels*, check out the CliffsNotes Resource Center.

CliffsNotes provides the following icons to highlight essential elements of particular interest:

Reveals the underlying themes in the work.

Helps you to more easily relate to or discover the depth of a character.

Uncovers elements such as setting, atmosphere, mystery, passion, violence, irony, symbolism, tragedy, foreshadowing, and satire.

Enables you to appreciate the nuances of words and phrases.

Don't Miss Our Web Site

Discover classic literature as well as modern-day treasures by visiting the CliffsNotes Web site at www.cliffsnotes.com. You can obtain a quick download of a CliffsNotes title, purchase a title in print form, browse our catalog, or view online samples.

You'll also find interactive tools that are fun and informative, links to interesting Web sites, tips, articles, and additional resources to help you, not only for literature, but for test prep, finance, careers, computers, and Internet too. See you at www.cliffsnotes.com!

LIFE AND BACKGROUND OF THE AUTHOR

Early Years and Education 2

Career 2

Major Literary Works 3

Early Years and Education

Jonathan Swift was born into a poor family that included his mother (Abigail) and his sister (Jane). His father, a noted clergyman in England, had died seven months before Jonathan's birth. There is not much known of Swift's childhood, and what is reported is not always agreed upon by biographers. What is accepted, however, is that Jonathan's mother, after the death of her husband, left the children to be raised by relatives (probably uncles), while she returned to her family in England (Leicester). It is also reported that Swift, as a baby, was taken by a nurse to England where he remained for three years before being returned to his family. This is open to conjecture, but the story contributes to the lack of information available regarding Swift's childhood.

Beginning in 1673, Swift attended Kilkenny Grammar School, where he enjoyed reading and literature and excelled especially in language study. In 1682, Swift entered Trinity College where he received a B.A. by "special grace," a designation for students who did not perform very well while there. Upon leaving Trinity College, Swift went to England to work as a secretary (a patronage position) for Sir William Temple. In 1692, Swift received an M.A. from Oxford; in 1702, he received a D.D. (Doctor of Divinity) from Dublin University.

Career

From approximately 1689 to 1694, Swift was employed as a secretary to Sir William Temple in Moor Park, Surrey, England. In 1694, he was ordained as a priest in the Church of Ireland (Anglican Church) and assigned as Vicar (parish priest) of Kilroot, a church near Belfast (in northern Ireland). In 1696, he returned to working with Sir William Temple, and in 1699, after the death of Sir William, he became chaplain to Lord Berkley.

In 1700, Swift became the Vicar of Laracor, Ireland, and he was also appointed prebend (an honorary clergyman serving in a cathedral) at St. Patrick's Cathedral in Dublin. In 1707, Swift was appointed as an emissary to the Church of Ireland, and in 1713, he was appointed as Dean of St. Patrick's Cathedral in Dublin. Throughout all this time, and, indeed, after his appointment as Dean of St. Patrick's, Swift continued writing satirically in various genres, including both prose and poetry, using various forms to address different causes, including personal, behavioral, philosophical, political, religious, civic, and others.

Major Literary Works

Between the years 1696–99, Swift wrote two major works: *Tale of a Tub*, defending the middle position of the Anglican and Lutheran churches, and *Battle of the Books*, taking the part of the Ancients (those who believed in the superiority of the classics and the humanities) against the Moderns (those who upheld the superiority of modern science, modern scholarship, modern politics, and modern literature). In *The Mechanical Operation of the Spirit* (1704), Swift continues his satiric attack on both questionable religious views and questionable knowledge acquisition, particularly scientific knowledge. In *Argument Against Abolishing Christianity*, Swift shares his reactions to the Test Act, a law enacted by Charles II, requiring office holders to declare their allegiance to the king over the church. *The Journal to Stella* (1710–1713), a series of letters written by Swift to Esther Johnson and Rebecca Dingley, includes the poem "The Windsor Prophecy," a satirical attack on the person and personality of the Duchess of Somerset, Queen Anne's red-haired attendant who did not care for Swift because of disparaging remarks Swift had written about her family.

Swift is also recognized as a defender of Ireland. In *A Modest Proposal* (1729), a reaction to English commercial practices that negatively impacted Ireland, Swift wrote one of the greatest works of sustained irony in English or any other language. Instead of maintaining that English laws prevent the Irish from manufacturing anything to sell, he argues that the only items of commerce that the English don't restrict are Irish babies and reasons that the Irish would be better off as cattle to be butchered than as a colony to be starved by the English. *The Drapier's Letters* (1724) is Swift's response to the continued subjugation of all aspects of the lives of those living in Ireland by England. The *Letters* aroused so much opposition that the English offered a reward of £300 for the name of the author. Although the Irish knew that he had written the letters, they did not betray him. They made him a national hero instead.

In his most recognized novel, *Gulliver's Travels* (1726), Swift presents a satire on all aspects of humanity by pointing out the weaknesses, vices, and follies inherent in all human beings; the satire reaches its apex in Swift's comparison of Houyhnhnms (horses) and Yahoos (human-like creatures) in Book IV.

In 1727, Swift visited England for the last time. He was declared mentally incompetent in 1742 and died in October 1745, leaving his estate to charity.

INTRODUCTION TO THE NOVEL

Introduction 5

A Brief Synopsis .5

List of Characters 7

Character Map 9

Introduction

It is unusual when a masterpiece develops out of an assignment, but that is, more or less, what happened in the case of *Gulliver's Travels*. The Martinus Scriblerus Club, made up of such notables as Pope, Arbuthnot, and Gay, proposed to satirize the follies and vices of learned, scientific, and modern men. Each of the members was given a topic, and Swift's was to satirize the numerous and popular volumes describing voyages to faraway lands. Ten years passed between the Scriblerus project and the publication of the *Travels*, but when Swift finished, he had completed what was to become a children's classic (in its abridged form) and a satiric masterpiece.

Swift kept the form of the voyage book but expanded his target. Instead of simply parodying voyage literature, he decided to attack what he considered were people's most conspicuous vices. He makes the abstract become concrete. Ideas are metamorphosed into grotesque, foreign creatures; absurd customs are represented by absurd objects; and the familiar becomes new and surprising.

A Brief Synopsis

Gulliver's Travels is an adventure story (in reality, a misadventure story) involving several voyages of Lemuel Gulliver, a ship's surgeon, who, because of a series of mishaps en route to recognized ports, ends up, instead, on several unknown islands living with people and animals of unusual sizes, behaviors, and philosophies, but who, after each adventure, is somehow able to return to his home in England where he recovers from these unusual experiences and then sets out again on a new voyage.

Book I: When the ship Gulliver is traveling on is destroyed in a storm, Gulliver ends up on the island of Lilliput, where he awakes to find that he has been captured by Lilliputians, very small people—approximately six inches in height. Gulliver is treated with compassion and concern. In turn, he helps them solve some of their problems, especially their conflict with their enemy, Blefuscu, an island across the bay from them. Gulliver falls from favor, however, because he refuses to support the Emperor's desire to enslave the Blefuscudians and because he "makes water" to put out a palace fire. Gulliver flees to Blefuscu, where he converts a large war ship to his own use and sets sail from Blefuscu eventually to be rescued at sea by an English merchant ship and returned to his home in England.

Book II: As he travels as a ship's surgeon, Gulliver and a small crew are sent to find water on an island. Instead they encounter a land of giants. As the crew flees, Gulliver is left behind and captured. Gulliver's captor, a farmer, takes him to the farmer's home where Gulliver is treated kindly, but, of course, curiously. The farmer assigns his daughter, Glumdalclitch, to be Gulliver's keeper, and she cares for Gulliver with great compassion. The farmer takes Gulliver on tour across the countryside, displaying him to onlookers. Eventually, the farmer sells Gulliver to the Queen. At court, Gulliver meets the King, and the two spend many sessions discussing the customs and behaviors of Gulliver's country. In many cases, the King is shocked and chagrined by the selfishness and pettiness that he hears Gulliver describe. Gulliver, on the other hand, defends England.

One day, on the beach, as Gulliver looks longingly at the sea from his box (portable room), he is snatched up by an eagle and eventually dropped into the sea. A passing ship spots the floating chest and rescues Gulliver, eventually returning him to England and his family.

Book III: Gulliver is on a ship bound for the Levant. After arriving, Gulliver is assigned captain of a sloop to visit nearby islands and establish trade. On this trip, pirates attack the sloop and place Gulliver in a small boat to fend for himself. While drifting at sea, Gulliver discovers a Flying Island. While on the Flying Island, called Laputa, Gulliver meets several inhabitants, including the King. All are preoccupied with things associated with mathematics and music. In addition, astronomers use the laws of magnetism to move the island up, down, forward, backward, and sideways, thus controlling the island's movements in relation to the island below (Balnibarbi). While in this land, Gulliver visits Balnibarbi, the island of Glubbdubdrib, and Luggnagg. Gulliver finally arrives in Japan where he meets the Japanese emperor. From there, he goes to Amsterdam and eventually home to England.

Book IV: While Gulliver is captain of a merchant ship bound for Barbados and the Leeward Islands, several of his crew become ill and die on the voyage. Gulliver hires several replacement sailors in Barbados. These replacements turn out to be pirates who convince the other crew members to mutiny. As a result, Gulliver is deposited on a "strand" (an island) to fend for himself. Almost immediately, he is discovered by a herd of ugly, despicable human-like creatures who are called, he later learns, Yahoos. They attack him by climbing trees and defecating on him. He is saved from this disgrace by the appearance of a horse, identified, he later learns, by the name Houyhnhnm. The grey horse (a

Houyhnhnm) takes Gulliver to his home, where he is introduced to the grey's mare (wife), a colt and a foal (children), and a sorrel nag (the servant). Gulliver also sees that the Yahoos are kept in pens away from the house. It becomes immediately clear that, except for Gulliver's clothing, he and the Yahoos are the same animal. From this point on, Gulliver and his master (the grey) begin a series of discussions about the evolution of Yahoos, about topics, concepts, and behaviors related to the Yahoo society, which Gulliver represents, and about the society of the Houyhnhnms.

Despite his favored treatment in the grey steed's home, the kingdom's Assembly determines that Gulliver is a Yahoo and must either live with the uncivilized Yahoos or return to his own world. With great sadness, Gulliver takes his leave of the Houyhnhnms. He builds a canoe and sails to a nearby island where he is eventually found hiding by a crew from a Portuguese ship. The ship's captain returns Gulliver to Lisbon, where he lives in the captain's home. Gulliver is so repelled by the sight and smell of these "civilized Yahoos" that he can't stand to be around them. Eventually, however, Gulliver agrees to return to his family in England. Upon his arrival, he is repelled by his Yahoo family, so he buys two horses and spends most of his days caring for and conversing with the horses in the stable in order to be as far away from his Yahoo family as possible.

List of Characters

Lemuel Gulliver A traveler and an adventurer. Gulliver is the protagonist of the *Travels*. He is an observer of other beings and other cultures.

Golbasto Momaren Evlame Gurdilo Shefin Mully Ully Gue The Emperor of Lilliput. Swift uses the Emperor as an example of rulers who must always have some type of support before making a decision.

Flimnap Lord High Treasurer of Lilliput.

Reldresal A Lilliputian councilor, Principal Secretary of Private Affairs.

Skyresh Bolgolam High admiral of Lilliput, a counselor of the Emperor.

Slamecksan and Tramecksan Lilliputian political parties. The first represents the Low Heels; the second represents the High Heels.

Glumdalclitch The daughter of Gulliver's master in Brobdingnag. She acts as Gulliver's nurse and protector.

The King of Laputa Leader of Laputa. He is preoccupied with mathematics and music.

The Academy Projectors (Professors) Balnibarbian reformers who plan reforms without considering effects.

Munodi The Governor of Lagado, on Balnibarbi. He represents the traditionalists, who are opposed to the reformers.

The Struldbruggs A race of humans who age without dying; they are immortal, but their immortality has none of its supposed delights.

Houyhnhnms Superior, totally rational horses, who are the masters of the Yahoos.

Yahoos The repugnant anthropoids held in subjection by the Houyhnhnms.

The Grey Horse (The Master) Gulliver's master in the Country of the Houyhnhnms.

Character Map

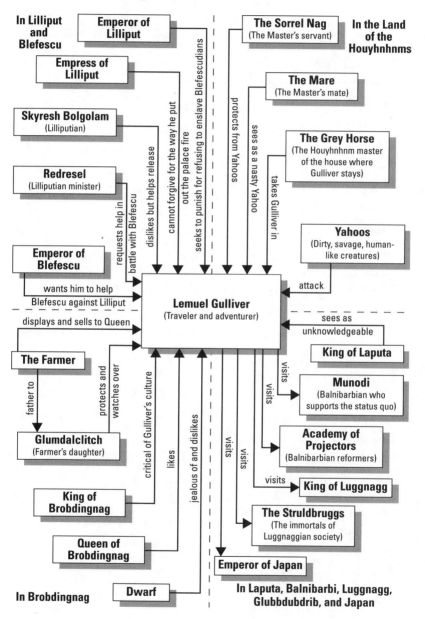

In Lilliput and Blefescu

Emperor of Lilliput

Empress of Lilliput

Skyresh Bolgolam (Lilliputian)

Redresel (Lilliputian minister)

Emperor of Blefescu

wants him to help Blefescu against Lilliput

requests help in battle with Blefescu

dislikes but helps release

cannot forgive for the way he put out the palace fire

seeks to punish for refusing to enslave Blefescudians

The Sorrel Nag (The Master's servant)

In the Land of the Houyhnhnms

The Mare (The Master's mate)

The Grey Horse (The Houyhnhnm master of the house where Gulliver stays)

protects from Yahoos

sees as a nasty Yahoo

takes Gulliver in

Yahoos (Dirty, savage, human-like creatures)

attack

displays and sells to Queen

Lemuel Gulliver (Traveler and adventurer)

sees as unknowledgeable

King of Laputa

The Farmer

father to

protects and watches over

critical of Gulliver's culture

likes

jealous of and dislikes

visits

visits

Munodi (Balnibarbian who supports the status quo)

Academy of Projectors (Balnibarbian reformers)

Glumdalclitch (Farmer's daughter)

King of Brobdingnag

Queen of Brobdingnag

visits

visits

visits

visits

King of Luggnagg

The Struldbruggs (The immortals of Luggnaggian society)

Emperor of Japan

In Brobdingnag

Dwarf

In Laputa, Balnibarbi, Luggnagg, Glubbdubdrib, and Japan

CRITICAL COMMENTARIES

Book I: A Voyage
to Lilliput 11
Chapter 1 11
Chapter 2 13
Chapter 3 15
Chapter 4 17
Chapter 5 19
Chapter 6 21
Chapter 7 23
Chapter 8 25
Book II: A Voyage to
Brobdingnag 27
Chapter 1 27
Chapter 2 29
Chapter 3 31
Chapter 4 33
Chapter 5 34
Chapter 6 36
Chapter 7 38
Chapter 8 40
Book III: A Voyage to
Laputa, Balnibarbi,
Luggnagg, Glubbdubdrib,
and Japan 41
Chapter 1 41
Chapter 2 43

Chapter 3 45
Chapter 4 47
Chapter 5 48
Chapter 6 49
Chapter 7 50
Chapter 8 51
Chapter 9 53
Chapter 10 54
Chapter 11 55
Book IV: A Voyage
to the Country of
the Houyhnhnms 56
Chapter 1 56
Chapter 2 58
Chapter 3 60
Chapter 4 62
Chapter 5 64
Chapter 6 65
Chapter 7 67
Chapter 8 68
Chapter 9 69
Chapter 10 71
Chapter 11 73
Chapter 12 75

Book I: A Voyage to Lilliput
Chapter 1

Summary

On this voyage, Gulliver goes to the sea as a surgeon on the merchant ship, *Antelope*. The ship is destroyed during a heavy windstorm, and Gulliver, the only survivor, swims to a nearby island, Lilliput. Being nearly exhausted from the ordeal, he falls asleep. Upon awakening, he finds that the island's inhabitants, who are no larger than six inches tall, have captured him. After the inhabitants examine Gulliver and provide him with food, the Emperor of this country orders his subjects to move Gulliver to a little-used temple, the only place large enough to house him.

Commentary

Character
Insight

In this first chapter, Swift establishes Gulliver's character. He does this primarily by the vast amount of details that he tells us about Gulliver. Clearly, Gulliver is of good and solid—but unimaginative—English stock. Gulliver was born in Nottinghamshire, a sedate county without eccentricity. He attended Emmanuel College, a respected, but not dazzling, college. The neighborhoods that Gulliver lived in—Old Jury, Fetter Lane, and Wapping—are all lower-middle-class sections. He is, in short, Mr. British middle class of his time.

Gulliver is also, as might be expected, "gullible." He believes what he is told. He is an honest man, and he expects others to be honest. This expectation makes for humor—and also for irony. We can be sure that what Gulliver tells us will be accurate. And we can also be fairly sure that Gulliver does not always understand the meaning of what he sees. The result is a series of astonishingly detailed, dead-pan scenes. For example, Gulliver *gradually* discovers, moving from one exact detail to another, that he is a prisoner of men six inches tall.

Concerning the political application of this chapter, note that Gulliver is confined in a building that was emptied because a notorious murder was committed there. The building probably represents Westminster Hall, where Charles I was tried and sentenced to death.

Glossary

(Here, and in the following sections, difficult words and phrases, as well as allusions and historical references, are explained.)

to alter my condition to marry.

hosier a haberdasher, a person whose work or business is selling men's furnishings, such as hats, shirts, neckties, and gloves.

four hundred pounds for a portion The part of a man's money or property contributed by his bride; here, meaning Gulliver's dowry.

East and West Indies East: Malay Archipelago; especially, the islands of Indonesia; West: the large group of islands between North America and South America; it includes the Greater Antilles, Lesser Antilles, and the Bahamas.

Van Diemen's Island former name for Tasmania.

declivity a downward slope or sloping, as of a hill.

several slender ligatures the ropes used to tie Gulliver to the ground.

buff jerkin a short, closefitting, sleeveless jacket or vest made of soft brownish leather.

durst dared.

hogshead a large barrel or cask holding from 63 to 140 gallons.

retinue a body of assistants, followers, or servants attending a person of rank or importance.

Signet Royal an official seal.

express a special messenger; courier.

soporiferous medicine medicine that causes or tends to cause sleep.

latitude angular distance, measured in degrees, north or south from the equator.

Chapter 2

Summary

In this chapter, the Imperial Majesty (the Emperor) and Gulliver carry on a conversation as best they can. After the Emperor's visit, six Lilliputians shoot arrows at Gulliver. Gulliver retaliates by pretending to eat the little archers and then releases them. This clemency, and Gulliver's cooperation, so impress the Imperial Council that they debate whether or not to free Gulliver. An officer takes inventory of Gulliver's possessions, which will be held until Gulliver's fate is settled upon.

Commentary

Swift makes the Lilliputians seem ridiculous by having Gulliver compare them to dolls. The little doll-like men strut and posture like full-sized men. Yet we cannot take them seriously. They are too tiny to be considered as majestic as they think they are. But "we" are not Gulliver, and *he* takes them seriously, especially the Emperor. Consider, for example, Gulliver's description of the Emperor: "His features are strong and masculine with an Austrian lip and arched nose, his complexion olive, his countenance erect, his body and limbs well-proportioned, all his motions graceful, and his deportment majestic." Everything that the Emperor does is respectfully detailed, which of course makes the scene even more entertaining and ridiculous.

Swift's contemporaries were doubtless amused by Gulliver's naive awe of the Lilliputian emperor. The Emperor's face clearly resembles the face of George I, yet Gulliver describes the assortment of features as handsome; George I was notoriously gross and ugly. Another political reference in this chapter concerns the list of things found in Gulliver's pockets. Normal, common, everyday possessions become unrecognizable when we see them out of proportion. To the Lilliputians, Gulliver's comb becomes a palisade. Swift is satirizing here the evidence presented against Harley and Bolingbroke in 1715. Certain Whig commissioners did their best to twist letters and books of the accused into treasonable meanings. Swift did not approve and described graphically the sinister distortions that party passion can cause in a person's mind.

Glossary

demesnes lands or estates belonging chiefly to a lord and not rented or let but kept in his hands.

draymen persons whose work involves hauling loads in a dray (a cart).

Chapter 3

Summary

The Lilliputian emperor is pleased that Gulliver is friendly and cooperative, so he rewards him with some court diversions. The diversions, however, prove to be quite different than one might expect. It is the Lilliputian court custom that men seeking political office demonstrate their agility in rope dancing, among other things. How long and how skillfully a candidate can dance upon a rope determines his tenure in office. Of the candidates, two are particularly adept: Reldresal, Gulliver's friend, and Flimnap, the treasurer. Other diversions include noblemen competing for official favor by crawling under or leaping over a stick, a feat for which they are then rewarded with various colored threads. Gulliver also reviews the Emperor's troops; he stands, legs apart, while the tiny men march through.

As a result of Gulliver's cooperation, a pact between Gulliver and the Emperor is agreed on. Gulliver is granted limited freedom on certain conditions. In return for abiding by the conditions, he will receive food sufficient for 1,728 Lilliputians. Gulliver swears to the articles in proper form, and the Emperor frees him.

Commentary

Theme

The jumping and crawling games that Gulliver describes sound innocent, like games children might play. Politically, however, their significance is far from innocent. The crawlers and jumpers perform for the amusement of the monarch and are rewarded with blue, red, or green threads. These threads represent the various orders of the Garter, the Bath, and the Thistle. George I used these orders as cheap ways of buying political support from social climbers. Politicians, Swift is saying, are always ready to debase themselves by performing humiliating games, hoping for colored ribbons, money, or titles.

Swift's model for Flimnap, the most dexterous of the rope dancers, was Robert Walpole, the leader of the Whigs. Walpole was England's first prime minister in the modern sense and an extremely wily politician. He resigned in 1717 but was restored to office four years later through the influence of the Duchess of Kendal. The Duchess was his mistress and, figuratively, is the cushion on which Flimnap breaks his fall. Walpole was not a pro-war Whig, but he did use war sentiment to retain power; privately, he believed that England prospered better under peace than war. Accordingly, Swift characterizes Flimnap's specialty as somersaults in mid-air. It is thought that Reldresal, the second most dexterous of the rope dancers, probably represents either Viscount Townshend or Lord Carteret. Both were political allies of Walpole.

The articles that Gulliver signs relate the political life of Lilliput to the political life of England. The first four articles seem to parallel the ancient position of the king of England. At one time, the king could not leave the country or enter London without permission. In addition, his writ was effective only on his royal domains and on the royal highways. It is possible that Swift is contrasting Gulliver, who is decent, with modern kings to suggest a contrast between antique virtue and modern degeneration.

The absurd and complicated method by which Gulliver must swear to the articles exemplifies another aspect of Whig politics: petty, red-tape harassing. The Whigs attacked the Tory's Treaty of Utrecht, maintaining that the peace treaty was invalid because the royal warranty was not properly countersigned. At the Lilliputian court, it is difficult for Gulliver to hold his right foot in his left hand and place the middle finger of his right hand on top of his head with the right thumb on the tip of his ear. Yet that is how he must "countersign" his agreement. If the thumb is not squarely on the ear, the sworn loyalty will be technically in question.

Glossary

summerset a somersault.

trencher a wooden board or platter on which to carve or serve meat.

colossus a gigantic statue.

pikes advanced a pike is a weapon used by foot soldiers, consisting of a metal spearhead on a long, wooden shaft; here, the weapons are held in an attacking position.

Chapter 4

Summary

After Gulliver's visit to the Emperor's palace at Mildendo, Reldresal, Lilliput's Principal Secretary of Private Affairs, pays a visit to Gulliver and explains the faction quarrels between the High Heel Party and the Low Heel Party. The conflict, he says, started over a religious question: At which end should the faithful break their eggs: at the big end or at the little end? The Blefuscudians break theirs, in the original style, at the big end. But, by royal edict, the Lilliputians must break their eggs at the little end. There are rebels in Lilliput, Reldresal says, and already 11,000 of them—Big Endians—have been put to death; others have fled to the court of Blefuscu. He explains further that the Lilliputians have lost 40 ships in the war. The dilemma seems hopeless, for Lustrog, the prophet of their religion, has said, "All true believers shall break their eggs at the convenient end."

Commentary

Gulliver's description of Mildendo gives Swift another chance to satirize the pretensions of the Lilliputians. The little people, for example, call their city a "metropolis"; Gulliver, however, describes the city as only 500 feet square. But he does not scoff at the Lilliputians; he accepts their self-declared importance. Thus, once again, Swift emphasizes the contrast between Gulliver's naive acceptance of the Lilliputian viewpoint and the physical facts he reports.

Theme

Swift also uses Gulliver's matter-of-fact tone to ridicule the religious war. Politically, Blefuscu stands for France and Lilliput for England. The war between the two over the religious question of egg-breaking symbolizes the long series of wars between Catholic France and Protestant England. The egg-breaking itself may refer to a quarrel over the nature of the sacrament, and it is also possible that it refers to the differences in communion of the Catholic and Anglican churches. The Anglicans receive communion by bread and wine; the Roman Catholics receive only bread. The French and English, of course, also fought over land and loot, but Swift is using the symbolic differences between churches to emphasize the absurdity of any religious war.

The reference to the grandfather of the present emperor, who cut his finger breaking an egg, is to Henry VIII. Henry broke with Rome over the question of papal authority and also over the matter of Anne Boleyn. The Big Endians are, therefore, Catholic, and the Little Endians are Protestant. The emperor who lost his life is Charles I. Charles supported Archbishop Laud and was accused of Roman Catholic sympathies. The emperor who lost his crown is James II, who tried to restore some of the rights of the Roman church. He also attempted to institute a standing army with Roman Catholic officers. Consequently, he was driven out of England in 1688.

Swift also relates the folly of the religious war between Lilliput and Blefuscu to immediate European politics. The two Lilliputian parties stand for English political parties. The High Heels represent Tories; the Low Heels, Whigs. The king was sympathetic to the Whigs. He used them to support Hanover against France and appointed them to official positions to strengthen his position against the House of Lords. Thus, as the Lilliputian emperor, he wears low heels. The Prince of Wales, later George II, surrounded himself with members of both parties who were out of favor. As a Lilliputian, he wears one high and one low heel and wobbles when he walks.

Glossary

garret the space, room, or rooms just below the roof of a house; attic.

damage to the pile a pile is a long, heavy timber driven into the ground to support a structure; here, meaning that Gulliver did not want to damage the structural support of the Emperor's palace by stepping in the wrong place.

fortnight a period of two weeks.

schism a split or division in an organized group or society, especially a church, as the result of difference of opinion, of doctrine, etc.

Chapter 5

Summary

Gulliver saves Lilliput from a Blefuscudian invasion by dragging the Blefuscudian ships to Lilliput. In gratitude, the Lilliputian emperor rewards Gulliver with the title *Nardac*. Gulliver is pleased with his new title, but he is not the Emperor's dupe. He rejects a plan to destroy Blefuscu completely and argues for a reasonable peace treaty. Gulliver's moderation in dealing with the Blefuscudians gives Flimnap and Skyresh Bolgolam a chance to slander him. The Emperor listens to the accusations and is cold to Gulliver when he grants him permission to visit Blefuscu in the future. Later, a fire in the palace breaks out, and Gulliver puts out the fire by urinating on it. There is a law against anyone passing water in the royal palace, however, and the Empress is so horrified by Gulliver's fire-fighting techniques that she never forgives Gulliver. The Emperor softens, though, and promises Gulliver a pardon for his crime.

Commentary

Here, Swift satirizes the War of the Spanish Succession: The Whigs had conducted a war against the Roman Catholic leaders of France and Spain. Although it had its religious over-tones, the war also involved trading rights with the colonies in America. The Tories, led by Harley and Bolingbroke, were willing to make a reasonable peace with France, and when they came to power, they immediately began to negotiate with the French. The result was the peace treaty signed at Utrecht in 1713. Their naval policy, they said, destroyed the Spanish fleet. The Whigs were unsatisfied. They maintained that it was Marlborough's infantry campaigns on the continent that had brought peace. Moreover, after the peace treaty was signed, the Whigs accused the Tories of treason because of a failure to get colonies and ports from France and Spain.

The fire-fighting episode may (or may not) refer to Swift's *Tale of a Tub*, which he wrote to defend the Church of England against its Puritan and Roman Catholic enemies. The book is satirical, often coarse, and Queen Anne was reportedly offended by Swift's coarseness. Because of this, she resisted his friends' suggestions that he be made a dean or bishop in England.

Glossary

encomiums formal expressions of high praise.

diuretic increasing the excretion of urine.

Chapter 6

Summary

Gulliver provides the reader with information regarding Lilliputian culture and the personal treatment that he receives from the Lilliputians. Regarding the Lilliputian system of laws, Gulliver says that treason is severely punished, which is not particularly surprising, but other laws are. These laws punish an unsuccessful accuser as severely as a traitor; fraud is most frequently punished with death; and any innocent man who is vindicated of a charge is rewarded. Interestingly, ingratitude is a capital offense. Moral, rather than clever men, are appointed to powerful positions, and atheists are barred from all government offices. Explaining the seeming contradiction between these good laws and the rope-dancing corruptions, Gulliver says that the latter were instituted by the present Emperor's grandfather.

The Lilliputians believe that parents marry out of sexual desire rather than love of children. Therefore they deny any filial obligation and establish public schools for children. Parents with children in school pay for each child's maintenance and are forced to maintain those that they breed. The schools for young nobles are spartan, and students are trained in honor, justice, courage, modesty, clemency, religion, and patriotism. The schools for tradesmen and ordinary gentlemen are like those of the nobles, but the duration of schooling is shorter. The Lilliputians educate women to be reasonable, agreeable, and literate. Workers and farmers have no schools.

Resuming his tale, Gulliver describes the visit of the Emperor and his family. They come to dine with Gulliver and bring Flimnap with them. The dinner proves to be a disaster because Flimnap, the royal treasurer, is appalled when he reckons the cost of feeding and housing Gulliver. What's more, Flimnap charges, his wife is attracted to Gulliver and has visited him secretly.

Commentary

Swift uses Gulliver's report of the Lilliputian laws and customs to illustrate a semi-Utopian society. He drew from such political theorists as Plato, in the *Republic*, and from More, in his *Utopia*, and he also used many of the suggestions of the political reformers and pamphleteers of his own day. His proposals were aimed at creating and enforcing moral virtue in the citizens.

Flimnap's charges against Gulliver parallel those made against Bishop Atterbury, a Jacobite, who was tried for treason in 1723. It is thought that the suspicions concerning Gulliver and Flimnap's wife refer to Walpole. Rumors about Walpole's first wife, Catherine Shorter, had accused her of misconduct, but Walpole displayed no concern. Flimnap is dishonored by his jealousy and Walpole by his complacency. If critics are correct about this parallel, Swift is unfair; he damns Walpole if he does, or if he doesn't, object. Also, of course, Swift is pointing out the absurdity of rash accusations made by politicians. Here, Gulliver is so much larger than the lady that she could not possibly have been unfaithful.

Glossary

concupiscence strong desire; lust.

his white staff domestic staff; housekeepers.

postillion a person who rides the left-hand horse of the leaders of a four-horse carriage.

Chapter 7

Summary

Gulliver learns that Flimnap, Skyresh Bolgolam, and others have approved articles of treason against him. His crimes include putting out the fire in the palace, refusing to devastate Blefuscu, speaking to the peace embassy from Blefuscu, and preparing to take advantage of the Emperor's permission to visit Blefuscu. The Emperor accepts the charges, but he refuses to kill Gulliver. Instead, he "mercifully" decides to blind Gulliver and save money on his upkeep by starving him slowly. On learning this, Gulliver escapes to Blefuscu.

Commentary

The Emperor's council that presses the charges against Gulliver stands for the commission of inquiry that preferred charges against the Tories. As a result of these charges, Harley and Bolingbroke were threatened with trials for treason. The first article, making water in the palace, may have reference to rumors that the Tories were sympathetic to Roman Catholicism. It may also apply to the charge that Harley and Bolingbroke treasonably and secretly revealed the instructions of the English negotiators to the French negotiators. The second charge correlates with overt attacks on the Tories for their refusal to continue the war and for their tries at negotiating a reasonable peace. The third charge stands for the accusation that Harley and Bolingbroke carried on secret correspondence with French negotiators. The fourth charge reflects the accusation that Harley and Bolingbroke intended to flee to France if their treason were discovered.

Swift uses this chapter to show that English politicians were bloody-minded and treacherous. In detail, he records the bloody and cruel methods that the Lilliputians plan to use to kill Gulliver; then he comments ironically on the mercy, decency, generosity, and justice of kings. The Lilliputian emperor, out of mercy, plans to blind and starve Gulliver. This plan seems a direct reference to George's treatment of some captured Jacobites. He executed them—after parliament had called him most merciful and lenient.

Glossary

the meanness of my condition my lowness in social status and rank; here, meaning that Gulliver was of humble origins and not of the nobility.

in a close chair in an enclosed, one-person chair with glass windows, carried on poles by two men; a sedan chair.

standing my trial facing my accusers.

Chapter 8

Summary

A few days after his arrival at Blefuscu, Gulliver sees a large overturned ship floating in the bay and hauls it to port. While he is restoring the ship for his return home, a Lilliputian envoy presents a note demanding that Gulliver be returned as a traitor. The Blefuscudian emperor refuses to do so, hoping that Gulliver will stay as a war deterrent between the two countries. Gulliver refuses, however, and sets sail for home. Eventually a British merchant ship picks him up and returns him to England where he is reunited with his wife and family.

Commentary

Gulliver's flight to Blefuscu recalls Bolingbroke's flight from England to France to escape the charges of treason pressed by the Whigs. The suggestions in the previous chapter that Gulliver might have pelted and destroyed the Lilliputian capital relate to Bolingbroke also. Supporters argued that had Bolingbroke and Harley actually intended treason, they could have revolted successfully. The Lilliputians' thirst for vengeance and their attempt to force the Blefuscudians to surrender Gulliver coincide with English protests against the Jacobites who found sanctuary in France.

Theme

By the end of Book I, Swift has drawn a brilliant, concrete, and detailed contrast between the normal, if gullible, man and the diminutive but vicious politician; the politician is always a midget alongside Gulliver. Swift makes it clear that the normal person is concerned with honor, gratitude, common sense, and kindness. Swift, however, is not through with comparisons. The representative person is a midget compared with the truly moral person. Swift prepares to send gullible Gulliver off on a voyage to a realm where practical morality works. The inhabitants of this realm are as much bigger than normal people as normal people are bigger than politicians.

Glossary

cordage cords and ropes collectively, especially, the ropes in a ship's rigging.

cabal a small group of persons joined in a secret, often political, intrigue.

young princes of the blood the nobility; here, meaning the succession of royalty.

the lee-side of the island the side or direction away from the wind.

ancient an ensign, or flag.

a bowling green at Greenwich a smooth lawn at Greenwich, a borough of Greater London.

the Black Bull in Fetter Lane a place of business (possibly a pub) leased by Gulliver.

leaving my family upon the parish leaving my family with no income; here, meaning Gulliver provides financial support for his family before leaving on his second voyage.

towardly child a friendly child.

Surat a seaport in western India, on the Arabian Sea.

Book II: A Voyage to Brobdingnag
Chapter 1

Summary

Gulliver is home for only two months when he and the crew of the *Adventure* set sail for Surat. A storm blows their ship far off course. When they finally sight land, the captain sends a crew, including Gulliver, to explore. While the crew looks for drinking water, Gulliver explores another part of the island. The men are set upon by "a huge creature" that chases them into the ocean and back to their ship. Gulliver, who was investigating the shore of the new country, is left behind. Eventually, Gulliver is discovered by several of these huge creatures that are, in reality, very large (giant-like) human beings. These giants prove to be friendly and curious, and eventually one of the giants, a farmer, takes Gulliver to his farmhouse where the farmer's friendly family receives him.

Commentary

When Gulliver finds himself in Brobdingnag, Swift first sets up the size ratio. Now the tables are turned: The Lilliputians were midgets one-twelfth Gulliver's size. Now Gulliver is a midget, and the giants who inhabit Brobdingnag are twelve times Gulliver's size. Besides the size change, notice too that Swift changes perspective in another way. When Gulliver was living among the Lilliputians, he described them as being like "little men." The Brobdingnagians who capture Gulliver, however, do *not* think of Gulliver as a "little man" or as a "little Brobdingnagian." Some of his first Brobdingnagian acquaintances think of him as being weasel-like or like dangerous and repulsive vermin. Thus Gulliver, in retrospect, seems more humane than we might have realized. To him, the Lilliputians were never insects or vermin, no matter how odious they acted. The Brobdingnagians are a contrast; they like him, generally speaking, but he is never a man. He is a plaything, a rare pet, but never a man.

Character Insight

If the Brobdingnagians do not see Gulliver as a man, however, we cannot condemn them on this one count. They are a moral people, and, again and again, Gulliver will show us instances of their moral virtue. But, at the same time, he never lets us forget that they are also aliens. He admires their laws, but he cannot abide their display of vast areas of flesh. He records his disgust at their physical selves in detail because he cannot overlook, or dismiss, magnified pores and moles and stray hairs. Our own flesh, however, would be repugnant—even to us—if we were to see it through the eyes of a doll-sized man. Yet they are flesh, and we are flesh, and it is this common bond that we, and Gulliver, share with the giant Brobdingnagians. They are a positive race of people, and even if we might not be able to attain their superior morality, we might profitably try to emulate certain of their standards.

Glossary

the Line the equator.

ague a fever, usually malarial, marked by regularly recurring chills.

arch boy a clever, crafty boy.

hanger a short sword, hung from the belt.

lappet a loose flap or fold of a garment.

scabbard a sheath or case to hold the blade of a sword.

sorrel any of various short, coarse weeds.

Molucca Islands group of islands of Indonesia, between Sulawesi & New Guinea.

Chapter 2

Summary

Of all the family, the farmer's daughter is the most fascinated by Gulliver. He seems like a walking, talking doll to her. She enjoys caring for him and even gives him a new name: Grildrig. She takes such good care of Gulliver that he calls her his *glumdalclitch* (nurse). News of Gulliver's living at the farmer's house spreads quickly, and several visitors come to see him. At the urging of one particular gentleman, the farmer decides to take Gulliver to the market place and to put him on display for others to see (for a price). This being successful, the farmer decides to take Gulliver on tour throughout the kingdom, including visiting the kingdom's metropolis, *Lorbrulgrud.* There Gulliver performs ten times a day for all who wish to see him. By this time, though, Gulliver has presented far too many performances; he is almost dead with fatigue.

Commentary

In this chapter, Swift demonstrates that the giants are kind and decent. It is a delicate process because, on the surface, Gulliver *seems* to be mistreated, yet the farmer is careful with Gulliver, and Glumdalclitch (Gulliver's name for the daughter) is especially loving with him. The farmer, it is true, almost kills Gulliver out of thoughtlessness, but he is never cruel or malicious to Gulliver (as the Lilliputians were). No normal Brobdingnagian is malicious; only children and the deformed are of that temper. These giants are not perfect; they are akin to us. Even the best of us are, sometimes, thoughtless and greedy. As for the rest of us, we are sometimes malicious—like the Lilliputians.

There is a stray political comment in this section that is of interest. Gulliver notes that the King of England himself would have felt isolated and different were he to be in a foreign land. This statement refers to George I. The English, and especially the Tories, made much of George's German origin.

Glossary

manikin (mannequin) a little man; dwarf; here, being a translation of the name *Grildrig*, the name given to Gulliver by the farmer's daughter.

pillion a cushion attached behind a saddle for an extra rider.

gimlet-holes holes made by a gimlet, a small boring tool with a handle at right angles to a shaft having at the other end a spiral, pointed cutting edge; here, meaning the holes bored in Gulliver's traveling box.

the Sign of the Green Eagle an inn where Gulliver performed.

Ganges a river in northern India, flowing from the Himalayas into the Bay of Bengal.

Chapter 3

Summary

The Queen asks for an audience with the farmer and Gulliver, and Gulliver performs admirably and respectfully for her. The Queen, being attracted to the novelty of this tiny man, buys Gulliver from the farmer. Included in this arrangement is the farmer's daughter, Glumdalclitch, who becomes a member of the Queen's court as Gulliver's nurse. Conversing with the King, Gulliver tells him about English customs and politics. The King is amused; he laughs at the fierceness of such tiny insects. Gulliver dares not refute the King's opinion; indeed, before long, he adopts his host's point of view.

The King and Queen are happy with Gulliver, but there is one member of the royal entourage who is *not* happy: the Queen's dwarf, who is jealous because Gulliver has replaced him in the Queen's affection.

Commentary

Swift prevents us from idealizing the giants by reminding us of their incapacity to accept Gulliver as a scaled-down version of a Brobdingnagian. Gulliver always considered the Lilliputians as miniature men, but this is not true of the Brobdingnagians. Even the King, who is affectionate towards Gulliver, thinks of him as rat-like and as a contrivance made of clockwork.

The King discredits Gulliver and his fellow Englishmen. And, because the King is adamant toward the English, Swift has a mouthpiece to voice some of his complaints. The English, he emphasizes, are contradictory. They "love, fight, dispute, cheat, and betray." In general, the Brobdingnagians do not. Interestingly, the only real "villain" in Brobdingnag is the Queen's jester—a dwarf, diminutive physically and lacking in the Brobdingnagian virtues, who wedges Gulliver into the hollow of a bone and dumps him into a large silver bowl of cream.

Theme

The King also mocks human pretension, and once again we recall our perspective. In Book I, we stood tall, like Gulliver, and watched the Lilliputians mimic human posturings and vanities. Now we stand small, like Gulliver, and listen to a moral giant discredit human pride and pretense. Gulliver accepts the King's judgment. Actually, it would be false pride not to. The King is merely telling Gulliver, and us, what we already know about the damage that results from inflated pride. But Gulliver is still gullible; his acceptance of the King's viewpoint reflects the fact that he is beginning to adjust to the Brobdingnagian perspective.

Glossary

scrutore (escritoire) a writing desk or table.

equipage furnishings; accessories.

Chapter 4

Summary

When the King and Queen go traveling about the country, they decide to take Gulliver along. Gulliver describes the island, the sea around the island, the city of Lorbrulgrud, the King's palace, his [Gulliver's] method of travel on the island, several of the island's inhabitants, and some of the sights to see on the island. In describing the inhabitants of the island, Gulliver focuses on their illnesses and diseases. He mentions, for instance, giant beggars, horribly deformed, with lice crawling all over them. Gulliver compares the sights to similar sights in his homeland. Finally, the dimensions of the King's palace are described with the kitchen receiving particular attention.

Commentary

The exact dimensions that Gulliver enumerates in the chapter emphasize Gulliver's smallness. The description of the church, for example, reinforces this notion: Size denotes morality. Swift also shows us another magnified view of human flesh. Gulliver sees people with obvious tumors and cysts, and he states, "But the most hateful sight of all was the lice crawling on their clothes: I could see distinctly the limbs of these vermin . . . ." Gulliver's interest as a doctor is piqued because he suggests that he would like to dissect one of these vermin, but he adds, ". . . the sight was so nauseous, that it perfectly turned my stomach." Even if we have disgust for the physique of the giant beggars, it is surpassed by our disgust for the lice that crawl over the enormous bodies. The lesson is this: The giant beggars may be physically revolting, but the pernicious little vermin (humans) are even more so.

Glossary

wen a benign skin tumor, especially of the scalp, consisting of a fatty cyst.

in battalia in full battle dress.

Chapter 5

Summary

Gulliver's mishaps continue. The Queen's dwarf drops barrel-sized apples on him; hailstones as big as tennis balls batter and bruise him; a bird of prey nearly grabs him; and a spaniel picks him up in his mouth and carries him to the royal gardener. Gulliver is insulted to be coddled and played with by the maids of honor. To them, Gulliver is a toy, not a man, so they undress in front of him without a thought of modesty. The maids, perhaps comely enough, repulse Gulliver. He is particularly annoyed when they titillate themselves with his naked self.

Because Gulliver is a sailor, the Queen has a toy boat made for him and a trough in which to sail. The royal ladies also take part in the game and make a brisk breeze with their fans. Disaster strikes when a frog hops into the trough and nearly swamps Gulliver's boat, but Gulliver bravely drives the monster off with an oar. One day a monkey seizes Gulliver and carries him to the top of the palace. Gulliver is finally rescued and, when he recovers, is summoned by the King, who is curious to know whether Gulliver was afraid. Gulliver boasts that he could have protected himself with his sword. The King guffaws at the little *splacknuck's* pride.

Commentary

Gulliver has begun to accept the Brobdingnagian point of view, but Swift will not let him forget that he is *not* a giant. He may adopt certain ideas of the giants, but once Gulliver begins to have pretensions, he is literally knocked down to size. The mishaps with the hailstones, the spaniel, and the mole hole he falls into are not really serious, but they serve to discipline him. He is humiliated; none of them could have happened to a giant.

The humiliating incidents multiply. After a series of physical threats, Gulliver's emotional make-up is attacked. The maids of honor treat him as a plaything. They strip him and are curious about his maleness, but they ignore his masculinity. They offend his sexual pride by treating him as though he has no sexual significance. Then, in the abduction scene, Gulliver is likened not to a toy, but to a baby monkey. Swift continues to reinforce Gulliver's connection with animal smallness. The progression has been handled with great care. Gulliver's life was imperiled, his safety was endangered, his sexual pride was assaulted, and now he has been reduced to being monkey-like. Despite all, though, Gulliver is still tempted to brag about himself. He is still not aware that the giants are morally superior.

Glossary

Bristol barrel a barrel made in Bristol, England.

kite any of various birds of prey (e.g., hawks, eagles) with long, pointed wings and usually a forked tail.

espalier a lattice or trellis on which trees and shrubs are trained to grow flat.

cudgel a short, thick stick or club.

linnet a kind of small finch.

three tuns a tun is a large cask, especially for wine, beer, or ale.

wherry a light rowboat used on rivers.

varlet a scoundrel; knave.

Chapter 6

Summary

Gulliver entertains himself and demonstrates his ingenuity by using the King's beard stubble to make a comb and by using strands of the Queen's hair to make several chairs and a purse. In addition, Gulliver plays the spinet (piano) for the King and Queen by using sticks formed as cudgels to bang on the keys as he runs up and down a piano bench. The King also holds several audiences with Gulliver to discuss the culture of Gulliver's home country, England. In these audiences, as requested by the King, Gulliver explains the role of the people in the operation of the government, in religion, and in the legal system, among other topics. The King, after asking many questions related to all that Gulliver tells him, concludes this audience with a summary and an assessment of what he hears.

Commentary

In this chapter, Swift changes his focus to European politics and institutional morality. The king is the questioner, and Gulliver is the "expert." Immediately we sense that what Gulliver says is naive. He is idealizing his country's customs and institutions; he even lies about them. His distortion, therefore, is revealing: It exposes the actual workings of the English system.

Besides attacking the English as a whole, Swift singles out the Whigs. When the King asks whether lords are advanced because of achievement or from political convenience, the reference is to the Whigs' buying votes in parliament by granting nobility to politicians. When the King asks whether bishops are ever appointed because of their political opinions, the reference is again to the Whigs, who appointed writers of their party to bishoprics. Conversely, clerical success was denied Swift largely because of his political opinions. When the King asks whether members of parliament are not sometimes elected by bribery or influence, the allusion is to Walpole, a master at rigging elections. And when the King asks whether judges don't sometimes get rich and dispense partial and slow justice, Swift's inference is that justices of the peace are usually stupid and biased and that judges in the higher courts are notoriously slow and usually very rich.

Style & Language

Swift has Gulliver invoke the rhetoricians before he begins praising England; then he connects this highly formal invocation with the ludicrous spectacle of Gulliver proudly banging on the piano with mallets. Also, Swift uses insect imagery to surround the discussion of the morality of Europe; Gulliver even brags that bees and ants have a reputation for sagacity. Gulliver's praise rings hollow. The King tells his pint-sized performer that English history is not as Gulliver describes; rather, it is a "heap of conspiracies, rebellions, murders, massacres, revolutions, banishments, the very worst effects that avarice, faction, hypocrisy, perfidiousness, cruelty, rage, madness, hatred, envy, lust, malice, or ambition could produce." He concludes that the bulk of Gulliver's countrymen are "the most pernicious race of odious little vermin that nature ever suffered to crawl upon the surface of the earth."—a statement that is not only the most famous statement in the *Travels*, but is perhaps the most famous in all literature in its assessment of the nature of mankind.

Glossary

the King's levee a morning reception held by a sovereign or person of high rank upon arising.

awl a small, pointed tool for making holes in wood, leather, etc.

consorts seventeenth-century English chamber music ensembles, sometimes including vocalists.

spinet an early, small variety of harpsichord with a single keyboard.

play a jig to perform a fast, gay, springy sort of dance, usually in triple time.

sifted me to inspect or examine with care, as by testing or questioning; here, meaning the King asked many probing questions of Gulliver.

chancery the court of the Lord Chancellor of England.

gaming the act or practice of gambling.

Chapter 7

Summary

Gulliver decides that the King's lack of enthusiasm for England springs from his ignorance of the country. To remedy this, Gulliver offers to teach the King about England's magnificence. The first lesson concerns one of England's most valuable assets: gunpowder. Describing its effects graphically and at great length, Gulliver tells the King that gunpowder would be a great boon for him; with it, the King could reduce all his subjects to slavery. The King is horrified by the suggestion. He rejects such a bloodthirsty and inhumane proposal, warning the "impotent and groveling insect" (Gulliver) that he will be executed if he ever mentions gunpowder again.

Gulliver drops the subject of gunpowder and gives us an account of the customs and government of his hosts. The Brobdingnagian army is a national guard or militia; there are no professional soldiers. As for government, it is extremely simple. There are no refinements, mysteries, intrigues, or state secrets. Government depends upon common sense, mercy, and swift justice. Brobdingnagian learning consists only of morality, history, poetry, and practical mathematics. The Brobdingnagians cannot understand abstract reasoning or ideas. Their laws must contain only twenty-two words and must be absolutely clear. Their libraries are small, and their books are written in a clear style.

Commentary

Character
Insight

Swift shows us that Gulliver's character seems to be changing for the worse. His pride is growing to enormous proportions; he becomes condescending to the King. He calls the King a nobody and says that the King's standards are not worthy of emulation: "But great allowances should be given to a king who lives wholly secluded from the rest of the world and must, therefore, be altogether unacquainted with the manners and customs that most prevail in other nations: the want of which knowledge will ever produce many prejudices, and a certain narrowness of thinking, from which we (England) and the politer countries of Europe are wholly exempted." He then waxes patriotic and political over European morality, mentioning Dionysius of Halicarnassus. Significantly, Dionysius was a partisan historian who lied when it suited his purpose. He also sneers at the King's idea that government should be compounded of common sense, justice, mercy, and understandable laws. Yet, the laws and customs that the King describes are ideal; most of all, they are sensible. They are not abstract or transcendental. They serve to keep people honest, happy, and free.

Literary Device

Instead of censuring the Whigs, most of Swift's allusions in this section draw attention to English intellectual follies. Gulliver remarks that he could not teach the giants to think in abstractions and transcendentals; instead their thinking was always clear. This observation anticipates Swift's ridicule of the Modern philosophers in Book III. Swift is saucy on the subject of the "Moderns." Already in his *Battle of the Books,* he berated certain poets, philosophers, and scientists who called themselves the "Moderns." This group cited gunpowder as evidence of Modern superiority over the Ancients and also praised Modern philosophers who used abstract and transcendental terms.

Swift's mention of the giants who preceded the smaller Brobdingnagians reminds us that the Brobdingnagians are not perfect, but they are consistently moral. They still have a remnant of their former greatness. There is prosperity and peace, morality and common sense in Brobdingnag.

Glossary

transcendentals philosophers who propose to discover the nature of reality by investigating the process of thought rather than the objects of sense experience.

Chapter 8

Summary

Gulliver spends two years in Brobdingnag, but he is not happy despite the royal family's pampering. He is afraid that he will never escape and will turn into a sort of domestic, albeit royal, pet. Escape seems impossible; chance, however, intervenes: On a trip to the seashore, an eagle swoops down, snatches up the box Gulliver travels in, and drops it into the sea. The box is driven by the wind close to an English ship and is spied by some sailors, who retrieve Gulliver and his possessions. Gulliver does not adjust easily to his fellow Englishmen. After living two years in a land of giants, he has convinced himself that all Englishmen are midgets. Everything looks tiny back home, and he feels like a giant. In time Gulliver's sense of perspective heals.

Commentary

Character Insight

Swift reinforces the idea of the giant's moral superiority by having Gulliver identify the English with the Lilliputians. This association also makes Gulliver ridiculous. It demonstrates the folly and self-deception that Gulliver practices in identifying himself with the moral giants. Gulliver's pride is at the root of his trouble. Swift dramatizes this with the mirror Gulliver cannot bear to look into. The mirror is a standard device, just as satire is; anyone who looks closely is shown his own flaws.

Swift has finished his commentary on human morality. In Gulliver's next voyage, he trains his satire on people's intellect: how they use—and misuse—it.

Glossary

hundred leagues one league is about three nautical miles; here, meaning about 300 nautical miles.

conceit an idea, thought, concept.

raillery light, good-natured ridicule or satire; banter.

Book III: A Voyage to Laputa, Balnibarbi, Luggnagg, Glubbdubdrib, and Japan
Chapter 1

Summary

Gulliver stays home only a few months before shipping out to sea again, as ship's surgeon, on the *Hopewell*. On reaching the port of Tonquin, the captain appoints Gulliver and a crew of fourteen to take a sloop loaded with other goods to trade with some nearby islands, but after a few days of sailing, a storm drives the sloop far off course. To compound the problem, pirates attack and capture Gulliver and his crew. Gulliver, as captain, is set adrift, and he spies a great object in the sky, an object which appears to be a flying island. The people on the Flying Island drop a seat attached to a chain to Gulliver, and he, welcoming this rescue, is lifted aboard.

Commentary

By comparing the malicious Dutchman to the relatively merciful pagan pirates, Swift begins a sustained disparagement of the Dutch. The Dutchman betrays a fellow Christian out of greed and malice; he would like to have Gulliver killed, whereas the pirate, at least, spares Gulliver's life. Swift is setting up a contrast between the Dutchman whom we meet here (and those we meet later) and the charitable Portuguese captain whom we meet at the end of Book IV. The Dutch are convenient villains for Swift. Already, in *The Conduct of the Allies*, he had indicted them and the Whigs for their conduct of the war. The Dutch, it is true, had been allies of England in Marlborough's land campaigns against France, but they were allies chosen by the Whigs.

Literary Device

The flying island has a long history in satire. Many other satirists had used it as simply a marvel, but Swift takes it out of the realm of the incredible. He converts it from a marvel to a device; it is graphic and rather believable because we are told in great detail how it operates. Swift also makes it doubly useful by showing how the Laputans use it as an instrument of political tyranny.

Glossary

Levant region on the eastern Mediterranean, including all countries bordering the sea between Greece & Egypt.

Tonquin (Tonkin) the Gulf of Tonkin, an arm of the South China Sea between Hainan Island and the coast of southern China; here, the first port visited by the *Hopewell*.

pocket-glass a small telescope; spyglass.

pocket-perspective another type of spyglass.

supplicating postures requests for help, as in a prayer-like position. Gulliver is humbly seeking rescue by the flying islanders.

the verge the edge; here, meaning the edge of the Flying Island.

Chapter 2

Summary

Gulliver meets the inhabitants of the Flying (Floating) Island, learns that it is called Laputa, and immediately realizes that the inhabitants are a distracted people who have a very limited attention span and very narrow interests; their main concerns are essentially mathematics and music. Gulliver observes the Laputans. Their clothes, which do not fit, are decorated with astrological symbols and musical figures. They spend their time listening to the music of the spheres. They believe in astrology and worry constantly that the sun will go out. The Laputan houses, he notices, are badly built, without accurate right angles. The Laputan women are highly sexed and adulterous, preferring men from the island of Balnibarbi. The Laputan husbands, who are so abstracted in mathematical and musical calculations, don't know that their wives are adulterous.

Commentary

Theme

Here, Swift concentrates his satire on people's pride in reason. Reason, in Swift's era, was valued above all other faculties. Science was fast becoming a religion, with the telescope and the microscope as fountain-heads of Truth. Swift found this unnatural. He felt that too thorough an emphasis on reason obscured the human elements in a person's make-up. Even Swift's choice for the name of the flying island indicates his opinion of the Age of Reason. Gulliver explains to us what he believes *Laputa* to mean, but his speculations are wrong. The name *Laputa* comes from Spanish and means "the whore." We are reminded of Martin Luther's famous description of reason: "That Great Whore, Reason!" Luther became infuriated with reason because some of his opponents were using it to deny the Lutheran emphasis on faith. Swift was generally sympathetic to the Lutheran adherence to faith and the system of morality built upon it. By naming the island Laputa, he warns his readers that he is deprecating those rationalists and abstract reasoners who are antagonists of faith.

Character Insight

The Laputans are speculative and rationalistic philosophers. And they are dismal failures—as philosophers, as reasoners, and as men. They are devoted to the most ethereal of abstract disciplines—music and mathematics—but cannot play music well or figure accurately enough to build houses or tailor clothes. They are completely incompetent in practical affairs and don't even notice that their wives are notoriously unfaithful.

Swift uses the whoring wives of the Laputans to suggest that immorality accompanies abstract, proud reason. The story from Juvenal relates these licentious women directly with national morality and English politics. In addition, Swift also takes a poke at Walpole, the leader of the Whigs. The woman who runs away to live with a slave has reference to the stories that circulated about Walpole's wife.

Incorporating other political allusions, Swift chides George I by means of the Laputan's king's hospitality to Gulliver. George I was notorious for filling his administration with illiterate Germans from Hanover. The tailor's mistake in calculation applies to Isaac Newton, a mathematical theorist who dabbled in politics. Newton suffered ridicule because a printer made a mistake in one of the figures Newton used in computing the distance of the earth from the sun. Swift, however, had yet another quarrel with Newton. Newton recommended a scheme to debase Irish coinage that Swift believed was immoral and callous. Newton was a convenient model for Swift, who believed that he incorporated the essence of the immoral, abstract reasoning scientist. Swift also makes satirical use of the Laputan anxiety about the health of the sun and the comet theories. Many of his contemporaries were so interested in astrology, Swift believed, that they might worry over a comet and not notice their wives' infidelity.

Glossary

quadrant an instrument similar to the sextant, used by naivgators for measuring the angular distance of the sun, a star, etc. from the horizon.

gallants men attentive and polite to women.

caprices sudden, impulsive changes in the way one thinks or acts.

Chapter 3

Summary

Gulliver's explains how the Flying Island moves by giving what he calls "a philosophical account" of its movement capabilities. The explanation is quite complicated, but the movement principle is quite simple and is based upon magnetic forces in the Flying Island and in the country below (Balnibarbi). These forces, working in opposition, allow the island to move up, down, forward, backward, and sideways by means of using the attracting and repelling principles inherent in the science of magnetism. Gulliver also explains how the King uses the Flying Island to tyrannize the people of Balnibarbi. He can cut off sunshine and rain from any region on the lower island. Or, if he wishes, he can pelt it with stones. Theoretically, he could lower Laputa and crush Balnibarbian towns. Finally, Gulliver relates the story of the successful rebellion of the city of Lindalino.

Commentary

Literary
Device

Gulliver's description of the movement of the island is a parody of papers often delivered to the Royal Society. Swift is mocking the Society's fondness for concrete, technical language, and their love of mathematical and pseudo-mathematical diagrams. Gulliver's enthusiasm for the astronomical discoveries of the Laputans parodies the enthusiasm of the Royal Society for Halley's and other astronomers' observations of comets. It should be remarked, however, that Swift describes with great accuracy the two satellites of Mars. These satellites were not observed until 1877.

Swift fills his reader's mind full of reminiscences of scientific speculation with the description of the island. Then he proceeds to link these remembrances to political terrorism and tyranny. The King's attack on Balnibarbi, for example, and his policies toward Balnibarbi parallel the English crown's policies toward Ireland. Cutting off the rain and the sun refers to the royal policies that cut off Irish trade. The tall rocks in the towns of Balnibarbi seem to represent the Irish peers; the high spires represent Irish bishops, who protested Wood's scheme; and the pillars of stone probably characterize the Irish merchants.

Ireland was a rebel country and Lindalino, no doubt, represents Dublin. The towers Lindalino raised correspond to the grand jury that investigated Swift's *The Drapier's Letters*, the Irish privy council, and the two houses of the Irish parliament. The privy council and the parliament resisted Wood's scheme (that would debase Irish coinage), even at the cost of losing royal bribes. The lodestones installed to catch the island probably represent various quasi-legal organizations of merchants and citizens who opposed Wood's debased coinage. Swift's contemporaries seem to have recognized the many political references because the printers suppressed the Lindalino incident; it did not appear in the *Travels* until the nineteenth century.

Glossary

adamant a hard stone or substance that was supposedly unbreakable.

packthreads strong, thick thread or twine for tying bundles, packages, etc.

Chapter 4

Summary

Gulliver's discontent with being on this Flying Island increases, and so he is lowered to Balnibarbi where he visits Munodi, at one time the Governor of the city of Lagado. Munodi shows Gulliver around the island—and a most unusual island it proves to be. Except for Munodi's estate, which is flourishing and green, the land is completely eroded and barren. Munodi explains that everything changed after several people visited Laputa. These travelers came back dissatisfied with the way things were and established an "academy of PROJECTORS," the objective of the academy being to change the direction of all "arts, sciences, languages and mechanics" and "to contrive new rules and methods of agriculture and building." But none of their plans ever worked. Now the land is unproductive. Munodi's fields are bountiful because he follows the customs of his ancestors.

Commentary

Theme

In Balnibarbi, Swift discredits the kind of intelligence that is interested in the way things work without considering the ends to be attained. Here (and later) he stigmatizes the amoral engineer. All the projects that Gulliver describes are parodies of undertakings seriously advanced by English scientists. To illustrate the sterility of the engineering mentality, Swift has each experimenter reversing a natural process. Swift then illustrates the relationship between the engineering intellect (that reverses natural processes) and politics. Munodi, for instance, was a good civil servant who did his job well. He incurred national disgrace, however, when he failed to beat time well during a concert. His crime: He offended an abstraction—music.

Of all the Balnibarbians, Munodi alone is obedient to natural processes. In caring for his estate, he respects and follows the precepts of his ancestors; as a result, his estate flourishes. Those who listen to the "projectors" and the scientific experimentalists cause their land to become barren and desolate.

Chapter 5

Summary

Gulliver visits the Grand Academy to observe the many experiments that are being tried out. The intent of these projects is to improve some process, product, or human behavior for the good of humanity. Gulliver studies several projects in progress—for example, trying to extract sunshine from cucumbers, trying to reduce human excrement to its original food, and making gunpowder from ice, among others. In another room, there are language projects, one of which is an endeavor to abolish words altogether. Gulliver feels that none of the projects are yet perfect.

Commentary

In this chapter, Swift expresses a concern about the nature (and worth) of scientific study of undeserving things. Furthermore, each of the absurd projects that Gulliver reports in this chapter reverses a natural process. All the projects fail, and Swift exposes them as pointless and useless.

The Royal Society is also implicated by Gulliver's reference to the language project. The proposal to substitute objects for words is very much like an actual proposal made by Sprat, the historian of the Society. Sprat wanted the Society's reports to be written in a mathematically plain style—a style that would contain pictures of all the things mentioned; the style, therefore, would have almost as many pictures in it as words.

Glossary

human ordure human excrement.

calcine ice to burn ice into powder.

tincture a dye.

annual and diurnal motions active throughout the year and during the daytime; here, meaning the project required a time adjustment both yearly and during the day (because the project involved a sundial).

Chapter 6

Summary

Gulliver tells us that the political scientists he visits are quite insane. They have proposed that administrators be chosen for their wisdom, talent, and skill; that ability and virtue be rewarded; and that ministers be chosen for their love of public good. One scientist proposes to improve state business by kicking and pinching ministers so as to make them less forgetful. Another says that he would expose treasonous plots by examining excrement because people are most thoughtful on the toilet. Two measures for raising taxes are also advanced. The first would let one's neighbors decide on one's vices and follies and then set a tax on each offense. The second measure would allow each man to decide how seductive, witty, and valiant he was; and, each woman would decide how beautiful and fashionable she was. Then a tax would be imposed on seductiveness, wit, valor, beauty, and fashion. It is obvious to the Balnibarbians that all the professors are as mad as March hares.

Commentary

Here Swift lets the Balnibarbians condemn certain of their own people. The "insane" political scientists actually outline some of the moral remedies that Swift would recommend. In particular, Swift censures human vanity and malice by means of the methods devised to assess taxes. Swift also relates Balnibarbian politics to English politics. The theory that treason can be discerned by reading signs in excrement finds its English parallel in the trial of Bishop Atterbury for treason. Some of the evidence introduced against the bishop was taken from papers discovered in his bathroom.

Glossary

scrofulous tumours swellings of the neck glands.

cephalalgics medicines for the treatment of headaches.

icterics medicines for the treatment of jaundice.

apophlegmatics medicines for eliminating excess phlegm.

Chapter 7

Summary

Gulliver visits Glubbdubdrib, an island populated by sorcerers. The governor of the island, who can make people disappear or return from the dead, invites Gulliver to visit with several persons brought back from the dead. Thus Gulliver discovers that Alexander was not poisoned and that Hannibal did not use fire and vinegar to destroy an impassable boulder in the Alps. Caesar and Brutus are evoked, and Caesar confesses that all his glory doesn't equal the glory Brutus gained by murdering him. History, Gulliver considers, is not what it seems.

Commentary

Style & Language

Chapter 7 reads more like a collection of notes for a satire on the study of history than a carefully worked-out attack. While we do not know enough about the manuscript of *Gulliver's Travels* to say for sure, it does appear as though Swift had worked up notes for a satire on learning and history. Then, after having dropped the project, he seems to have picked it up again and inserted the notes into the *Travels*. We do know, for instance, that he wrote Book III last. Signs of this book's relatively hasty composition show up especially in his treatment of Gulliver. In this section, Gulliver is less complex than previously. He is not the gullible man who poses uncomfortable questions; rather, he seems to be just a visitor relating information about the curious customs of the natives.

Nevertheless, Book III *is* central to the *Travels*. In his satire on history and the historians, Swift refutes the claims made by historians and shows that politicians have degenerated, not progressed, when he compares the Roman senate and a modern parliament. Here, also, he demonstrates that reason is not trustworthy enough to supply a foundation for politics or morality. The way has been prepared for Book IV.

Glossary

a small convenient barque (bark) any boat, especially, a small sailing boat.

obeisances gestures of respect or reverence, such as a bow or a curtsy.

domestic spectres ghostly servants.

Chapter 8

Summary

Gulliver, continuing his interaction with those brought back from the dead, visits with Homer, Aristotle, Descartes (a French philosopher and mathematician), and Gassendi, (a French philosopher and scientist). He also spends several days visiting with Roman emperors and with several rulers whom he terms as "modern dead." He then focuses on modern history and is disappointed to find that these rulers have not been as virtuous as people have been led to believe. Finally, Gulliver asks to visit with some English yeomen; he is astonished to see that they are so sturdy. The race, he fears, has degenerated because of a rich diet and syphilis, and the current generation is as corrupt and degenerate as if they were nobles.

Commentary

Theme

Swift has attacked rationalistic and abstract thinking in Laputa and pragmatic and amoral scientific thinking in Balnibarbi. Now he lambastes the so-called humane studies of the Moderns, particularly the historians and philosophers. On the whole, Swift argues, poetry and ancient philosophy are more admirable than other ways of gaining knowledge because they teach morality and decency. Swift pits the ancient authors, like Homer and Aristotle, against their commentators. Most literary commentators and most historians, Swift asserts, distort those they write about. Swift points to Didymus and Eustanthius, ancient scholars who misread and misrepresented Homer. Then he singles out Scotus and Ramus, who, he says, misrepresented Aristotle. Such modern philosophers as Gassendi and Descartes were once popular; now they are unfashionable. Newton, Swift says, will also become unfashionable in his turn. His conclusion is that modern authors have no substance. He reduces them to matters of fashion, not truth.

After satirizing the humanities and philosophy, Swift turns to the historians. History, Swift infers, is the tool of politics; it is misread and miswritten for selfish reasons. In the service of politicians, history lies—about virtue, wisdom, and courage.

Glossary

the vortices of Descartes, were equally exploded in Descartes' philosophy, a vortex is a whirling movement about an axis, that accounts for differences in kinds of material bodies, etc.; the meaning here is that Descartes's philosophical positions were refuted.

helot a member of the lowest class of serfs in ancient Sparta.

royal diadems crowns.

Chapter 9

Summary

Gulliver journeys to Luggnagg posing as a Dutchman, but he is discovered and imprisoned. The King sends for Gulliver, and we learn about the King's idiosyncrasies. He requires those who have an audience with him to advance on their hands and knees and lick the floor. When a courtier is out of favor, the King sprinkles poison on the floor. (Sometimes after this ritual, Gulliver notes, the pages forget or carelessly neglect to sweep the floor. Such carelessness is fatal.) Gulliver follows the custom and, as a result of his willingness to answer questions posed by the King, Gulliver is invited to stay three months as a guest.

Commentary

Swift takes another slash at the Dutch by having Gulliver imprisoned merely because the Luggnaggians think that he is Dutch. He then unmasks the vanity of kings and the subservience of courtiers, using his usual technique of making abstractions concrete. He illustrates the subservience that the King demands and courtiers render by the ceremony of crawling and licking the floor. The moral—and physical—dangers of such subservience is shown by the poison on the floor. The King's mercy also falls under Swift's attack; the pages go "mercifully" unpunished for their occasional carelessness.

Glossary

fortnight a period of two weeks.

custom-house officer an agent in a building or office where customs or duties are paid and ships are cleared for entering or leaving.

Chapter 10

Summary

During his stay in Luggnagg, Gulliver hears about the *Struldbruggs,* people in Luggnagg society who are immortal. Gulliver's first reaction to hearing about the Struldbruggs' immortality is one of envy and enthusiasm because it would allow a person to gain immense wealth, wisdom, and the philosophical serenity. He fantasizes what he might do if he were one. However, when an interpreter explains the reality of life as a Struldbrugg—that is they grow old, feeble, decaying, and forgetful—Gulliver's enthusiasm for a life of immortality disappears as quickly as it began.

Commentary

In this chapter, Swift satirizes the theory that "experience is the best teacher." Already he has attacked all the other methods of gaining knowledge: Abstract reason was ridiculed in Laputa; pragmatic and scientific knowledge was his target in Balnibarbi; the humanities, and particularly history, suffered in Luggnagg. Now he discredits accumulated experience.

Like most people, Gulliver assumes that experience brings both wisdom and morality. He voices the human dream of immortality, sure that immortality will confer immense experience and, therefore, immense wisdom. Swift counters this naive dream of Gulliver's by presenting the Struldbruggs. It is true that they have immortality, but they do grow old. They wrinkle—and they degenerate; the physical is a symbol of the abstract once more. These creatures lack hope, kindness, generosity, affection, simplicity, honesty, and innocence.

Theme

When Swift's readers finish this chapter, they realize that Swift's theory is that reason is never to be exalted. People simply cannot depend on abstract, impersonal, inhuman reason. Nor can they depend on technological innovation, on history, or on the "modern" humane studies. The best guides are poetry and ancient philosophy.

Chapter 11

Summary

At last Gulliver is able to find a boat bound for Japan. In Japan, though, he finds himself in trouble again. It is customary for Dutchmen in Japan to trample the crucifix, and none have ever protested doing so. However, the Japanese emperor excuses Gulliver from this ceremony. Later, a Dutchman again tries to have Gulliver forced to trample on the cross. Gulliver leaves Japan on the *Amboyna*, bound for Amsterdam, and there he boards a ship for England. Finally he returns to his family in Redriff.

Commentary

The Dutch again come under attack in this chapter. They are meant to be a contrast to the charitable Portuguese captain who appears near the end of the *Travels*. Swift also compares the Dutch unfavorably to the Japanese, considered pagans in Swift's time. The Japanese have not nearly the malice of the commercial Dutch "Christians" and charitably allow Gulliver to escape this degrading ceremony by a subterfuge. They know he will be murdered by his Christian brethren if the truth is known.

Glossary

Redriff　Gulliver's family's home (estate).

the Downs　the locale of Gulliver's home in England.

Book IV: A Voyage to the Country of the Houyhnhnms

Chapter 1

Summary

After five months at home, Gulliver is offered and accepts the position of captain of the merchant ship. During the voyage, several of his crew become ill, and Gulliver is forced to hire replacements. Unfortunately, those hired are pirates who organize a mutiny on the ship and leave Gulliver on an island where he encounters a pugnacious, "odious" group of animals that look and act like primates and that attack him by climbing trees and defecating on him. Their attack ends when a horse appears on the road. This horse studies Gulliver with great curiosity and is soon joined by another horse, both of which seem to converse using words which Gulliver understands as *Yahoo* and *Houyhnhnm*.

Commentary

Style & Language

Gulliver's narration of his fourth voyage begins much as the others have. He uses a dry and matter-of-fact tone, and he offers a great deal of nautical detail. The style is deliberately prosaic. Swift is reaffirming Gulliver's unimaginative and credulous character. We can expect Gulliver to report what happens in Houyhnhnm land just as exactingly and as reliably as he does sailing dates, cargo information, and ports of call.

One other matter that might be noted before the adventure proper begins concerns the circumstances which have deposited Gulliver in the various foreign lands. Increasingly, these circumstances have become more serious. The sailors, in this section, maroon Gulliver out of treachery, malice, and ingratitude, whereas earlier he had been abandoned because of bad luck, fear, and greed. As Gulliver's mishaps become more threatening, the subject of each section becomes weightier.

Literary Device

Gulliver's description of the Yahoos displays one of Swift's most effective techniques: He describes the familiar in terms that are new. At first, the Yahoos seem familiar, but who, or what, they are is obscure. Then, with a jolt, Swift's point is obvious; the Yahoos are humans. Swift also captures the interest of his reader by posing a problem. He does not identify the Houyhnhnms as *rational* horses in this first chapter; therefore, the reader, like Gulliver, must try to solve the puzzle of who, or what, they are.

Character Insight

Gulliver describes the Yahoos as ". . . deformed . . . . Their heads and breasts were covered with thick hair . . . but the rest of their bodies were bare . . . . They had no tails and often stood on their hind feet . . . ." Then he adds, "I never beheld in all my travels so disagreeable an animal." The behavior of these animals is equally disgusting as Gulliver describes defending himself from them by drawing his sword and backing up to a tree for protection, but they then climb the tree and begin defecating on him. On the other hand, Gulliver's description of the horses, the Houyhnhnms, is almost idyllic: "The behaviour of these animals was . . . orderly and rational . . . acute and judicious." Indeed, it is a horse that rescues him from the Yahoos—not by any overt, physical action, but by simply appearing on the road—no physical action being necessary.

Glossary

Bay of Campeche an arm of the Gulf of Mexico, west of the Yucatan peninsula.

calentures any fever caused, as in the tropics, by exposure to great heat.

Leeward Islands a group of islands in the West Indies, extending from Puerto Rico southeast to the Windward Islands.

debauched led astray morally; corrupt; depraved.

expostulate to reason with a person earnestly, objecting to that person's actions or intentions.

sold the lading sold the (ship's) cargo.

pudenda the external genitals of the female.

dugs a female animal's nipples, teats, or udder.

Chapter 2

Summary

Gulliver, accompanied by the grey steed, walks to the grey's house where Gulliver meets several other Houyhnhnms. The grey (the master of the house) then takes Gulliver into a "court" where he observes several Yahoos eating roots and the flesh of "dogs and asses." Gulliver is placed near one of the Yahoos for comparison by the grey and his servant (a sorrel nag). Gulliver, at the same time, inspects the Yahoo standing next to him more carefully, and he realizes very quickly that the Yahoo has "a perfect human figure." As for the Houyhnhnms' reaction, the grey and his servant note that, with the exception of Gulliver's body covering (and his shorter hair and fingernails), he and the Yahoos are identical. Later Gulliver learns that his diet will consist of oats (naturally) that can be roasted, ground into flour, and mixed with milk to produce a kind of paste (an oatmeal) that he can eat. The grey also provides Gulliver with some temporary living quarters in a building near the stable.

Commentary

The contrast between the Houyhnhnms and the Yahoos is extreme. The horses are clean and sweet-smelling; their diet is temperate and vegetarian. Their habits constitute the temperance that the eighteenth century thought characterized reasonable man, stoics, and Adam before the fall. The Yahoos, on the other hand, are human in form and feature. They are filthy and they stink. They are omnivorous but seem to prefer meat and garbage. Significantly, they eat nearly everything prohibited by the biblical and Levitical food codes. Swift uses these details to make his comparison clear: the Yahoos' diet is depraved, whereas the horses' diet is like that of Man before the Fall.

Theme

Swift positions Gulliver midway—figuratively and literally—between the super-rational, innocent horses and the filthy, depraved Yahoos: Gulliver's home is midway between the stable house and the Yahoo pens. Gulliver lives an uneasy compromise with his nature. Physically, he is a Yahoo and only his clothes, thus far, prevent the horses from identifying him as a Yahoo. If the Houyhnhnms had recognized Gulliver as a Yahoo, Swift would have found it difficult to explain the way in which some of them accept Gulliver. Thus Gulliver's clothes are an excellent device for Swift. Because Gulliver's naked Yahoo-like self is hidden, Gulliver's identity is also hidden. Swift's point is that humans' basic difference from the Yahoo is largely artifice. Clothing— something artificial and extrinsic—"distinguishes" Gulliver.

Diet also places Gulliver midway between the Yahoos and the Houyhnhnms. He cannot live on oats alone. He must have some meat and some variety in his diet—the paste of grain and milk, for instance. Gulliver will try with admirable determination to improve himself; he will try to change himself into a more horse-like state, but he will fail. He is, simply, more of a Yahoo than a Houyhnhnm. His diet and his physique will prevent him from ever becoming a horse.

Swift uses Gulliver's character to establish a further point. Gulliver reacts to the Yahoos with immediate and overpowering detestation. He is horrified by the Yahoos' similarity to him. He lacks the humility to see himself as a sort of Yahoo. Rather, his pride leads him to try to become a horse. Yet Swift is saying that a person is not suited to become a "horse" (a dispassionate and virtuous stoic). Such dreams are as futile as Gulliver's belief that if he thinks hard enough he can acquire a fetlock or pastern.

Glossary

wattled built with wattles, a sort of woven work made of sticks intertwined with twigs or branches.

rack a box of some type for holding grain or some other commodity.

necromancy the practice of claiming to foretell the future by communication with the dead; here, meaning that Gulliver believes that this experience must be the result of some kind of magic—that it can't really be happening to him.

nag a horse that is worn out, old, etc.

hams the hocks or hind legs of a four-legged animal.

Chapter 3

Summary

Adept at languages, Gulliver learns rather quickly to talk with the Houyhnhnms. They speak a strange language, he says, yet it is similar to High Dutch. Besides the Houyhnhnms teaching Gulliver, he teaches them. They have no books, so Gulliver shows them how to write. The Houyhnhnms are truly mystified by their visitor; he seems to be so much like a Yahoo, but he also seems to be a rational Yahoo—a combination which they believe to be impossible. Gulliver describes for the Houyhnhnms the mutiny that stranded him, and they are astonished by the notion of a "lie." Horses, they say, do not even have a word for the concept of lying. They explain further that besides *Houyhnhnm* meaning "horse," it is derived from a word meaning "perfection of nature." Gulliver's Houyhnhnm host is curious about Gulliver's modesty. After all, he reasons, why would anyone want to conceal what nature has made? When he is naked, however, Gulliver looks *very* much like a Yahoo, so Gulliver's host promises to keep his guest's clothing a secret.

Commentary

Swift continues the theological implications he began with the dietary references in the first chapter. A Germanic scholar in the Renaissance had learnedly and earnestly proved that the language Adam and Eve spoke in paradise was High Dutch. Also, Charles V is supposed to have said that he would speak to his God in Spanish, his friend in English, his mistress in French, and his horse in German. The theory that Adam and Eve spoke German was familiar to Swift's audience. Milton had joked about it before Swift.

Character Insight

Swift has established the distinctions between Gulliver, the horses, and the Yahoos by using physical and concrete objects. He makes his point explicit by defining *Houyhnhnm*, which means "perfection of nature." This definition establishes an important distinction. The horses are uncorrupted by passion—either base or noble. They are devoid, for example, of charity. Also, they are not subject to temptation. Like Adam, they cannot understand the use of clothing. Swift never suggests that the Houyhnhnms stand for perfected human nature; on the contrary, they manifest *innocent* human nature. What they do—and what they say and think—*is* akin to human nature, but the character of the Houyhnhnms is far from Gulliver's. They are ignorant of many things which most people would consider venial. They cannot, for example, understand lying—or even the necessity for lying.

Swift thus establishes a range, or spectrum, of existence. The horses are literally innocent, having never (in theological terms) "fallen"; the Yahoos are super-sensual and depraved. The Houyhnhnms are ice-cold reason; the Yahoos are fiery sensuality. In between these extremes is Gulliver.

Glossary

glimmerings of reason   faint manifestations of rational thinking; here, meaning, that it might be possible for a Yahoo (Gulliver) to show some thinking ability.

prodigy   an extraordinary happening; here, meaning that a "brute animal" (the Yahoo, Gulliver) could show possibilities of being a "rational creature."

pastern   the part of the foot of a horse just above the hoof.

Chapter 4

Summary

Gulliver and his master continue their discussion of concepts that are difficult for the master to comprehend—especially those related to lying and doing evil. Gulliver explains the role of Houyhnhnms and the Yahoos in Gulliver's country, and, of course, the master is shocked when he learns how the roles are reversed. The master observes that the Yahoos in his land are better adapted for their lives than Gulliver. The master also compares the Houyhnhnms to the Yahoos and determines that the Houyhnhnm, as an animal, is much more functional than the Yahoo.

Commentary

Here, Swift begins to contrast the natural innocence of the horses with the depravity of the European Yahoos. He repeats the discussion about lying, thereby emphasizing the Houyhnhnms' uncorrupted reason; the horses cannot understand the nature of a lie.

Swift balances the earlier discussion of clothing by discussing the Houyhnhnm vocabulary. He infers that power, law, government, and punishment (words that have no equivalent in the Houyhnhnm language) are all artificial. Like clothing, which conceals and restructures the appearance of the body, these institutions restructure a people. They are Swift's moral equivalent of the physical clothing that the European Yahoo wears.

Swift attacks the legal profession by quoting many legal terms. The Houyhnhnms have no such words; natural virtue requires no lawyers. Besides being a satiric end in itself, this fun with words prepares us for the discussion of European social institutions.

Glossary

the least tincture of reason the smallest trace of reason; here, meaning that European Yahoos have no more ability to reason than do the savage Yahoos.

circumlocutions roundabout, indirect, or lengthy ways of expressing something.

Chapter 5

Summary

Describing England to his master, Gulliver talks at length about the bloody wars fought for "religious reasons"—Europeans, he says, will kill over whether flesh is bread or whether blood is juice or wine. Likewise, they murder each other out of jealousy for a government post. An invading prince, Gulliver says, will conquer a country, kill half the population, and make slaves of the rest, all in the holy name of civilization. Gulliver's master comments that, although *his* Yahoos are abominable, English Yahoos are far worse because they use their reason to magnify, yet excuse, their vices.

Gulliver then turns to the subject of England's legal system. The man in the right, he explains, is always at a disadvantage because lawyers are not comfortable unless they are arguing for the wrong side. In short, lawyers are the most stupid of all Yahoos; they are enemies to knowledge and to justice.

Commentary

Literary Device

In this chapter, Swift uses the technique of paradox as fuel for his satire. He gives paradoxical explanations for secular war, contrasting actual motives with professed motives. Swift is saying that men use their reason to give themselves *excuses*—instead of *alternatives*—for wars. Although we are not physically dangerous, we use reason to increase our power to kill. Swift concludes that as our reason increases so, proportionately, do our vices. From the gunpowder illustration, Swift moves to a social illustration: law and lawyers. The details he gives emphasize lawyers' antipathy to right reason: They destroy reasonable conversation, fight knowledge, and use reason to exalt injustice.

Glossary

culverins medieval muskets or heavy cannons.

carabines (carbines) rifles with short barrels (cavalry rifles).

Chapter 6

Summary

Gulliver discusses money and the difference between the poor and the rich. People lust for luxury, he says, but once they have it, it breeds sicknesses. And who treats the sick? Doctors—who can "magically" predict death because they can always kill their patients. Doctors, Gulliver laments, seldom cure. Gulliver then digresses to matters of state, citing a characteristic minister. This minister may gain an office by prostituting his wife or daughter. Or he may betray his predecessor. Or, hypocritically, he may attack government corruption.

Commentary

Money is stigmatized in this chapter as gunpowder was in the last. It is a medium whereby people can satisfy their vices and extend their misuse of reason. Swift draws on a theory that Bernard Mandeville made popular in his *Fable of the Bees.* Mandeville held that private vices increased business; thus private vices were public virtues. In Swift's view, private vices are no excuse for money-making; they constitute a vicious circle. To him, private vices are public vices.

Diet symbolizes these public vices which are pandered to by money. Great sums of money enable people to eat so-called gourmet foods in extravagant quantities. Such a diet is not necessary; indeed, it undermines health. Simple fare is far better. Yet expensive gourmet food is a status symbol. This artificially valued, unwholesome diet is thus paralleled with the naturally unwholesome fare of the Yahoos.

Style & Language

This chapter is one of the most complex, but one of the most unified, in the book. Swift starts with money and luxury, linking these to health and morality. He then uses doctors to associate disease with politics. Doctors can kill their patients; and the poisons that medicine has discovered can sometimes be "useful" to politicians. Finally, he links disease and luxury to the entire nation by describing the genetic defects and venereal diseases of the nobility, who marry for political and commercial reasons.

Glossary

repletion the state of having eaten and drunk to excess.

their natural bent their natural tendency or inclination.

intromission insertion.

obsequious and subservient showing too great a willingness to obey and be submissive; here, meaning that these are two characteristics of the behavior of ministers in relation to the princes who govern them.

rudiments of reason fundamentals of thinking; here, meaning that the Houyhnhnms felt that the Yahoo, Gulliver, might have the possibility of learning how to think.

Chapter 7

Summary

Impressed by the virtues of the Houyhnhnms, Gulliver decides to tell, freely and truthfully, as much as he can about Man. Gulliver has come to venerate the Houyhnhnms and hopes to be able to stay among them for the rest of his life. But Gulliver cannot be absolutely truthful; he extenuates people's faults and over praises their virtues. The more Gulliver tells, however, the more thoroughly he convinces his master that there are genetic and psychological links between humans and Yahoos.

Commentary

Swift sets up a point-by-point comparison between the Houyhnhnms' Yahoos and the European Yahoos he described earlier. He makes the moral flaws of Europeans vivid, concrete, and personal in the Yahoos. Yahoos collect stones as Europeans collect money. Yahoos fight among themselves like Europeans; their motive, like the Europeans' motive, is greed. They even have tribal politicians. The Yahoos get drunk and "howl and grin, and chatter, and reel, and tumble, and then fall asleep in the dirt." They are subject to melancholy and the "spleen"— fashionable complaints of rich Englishmen. For all their faults, however, the Houyhnhnms' Yahoos are not as vicious as the European Yahoos. What flaws the Yahoos have by nature, the Europeans increase and intensify through a perversion of their reason.

Glossary

sordid animal a dirty, filthy, squalid animal; here, meaning a Yahoo.

by rapine or stealth rapine: the act of seizing and carrying off by force others' property.

malicious insinuation an indirect and, in this case, spiteful suggestion or implication.

Chapter 8

Summary

Gulliver visits the Yahoos but cannot reconcile himself to their vulgarity. They eat frogs and fish and kennel in holes. They stink, cannot be housebroken, and hurl excrement at one another. When Gulliver goes swimming, he is cornered by one of the amorous females who embraces his naked body and, Gulliver says, would have sexually assaulted him had his protector, the Sorrel Nag, not saved him. In contrast to the Yahoos, the Houyhnhnms govern themselves wholly by reason. They take good care of their young, but they do it on the grounds of reason. Accordingly, they breed for strength and comeliness; no Houyhnhnm marries for either love or money. Also, there is no adultery. Once every four years, Gulliver tells us, the Houyhnhnms meet for an assembly to settle all problems. Not surprisingly, there are few or no problems that need solving.

Commentary

Houyhnhnms are a breed of moral animal, different from the Yahoos or Europeans. We have, in fact, already seen this difference in Chapters 3 through 6. Houyhnhnm society is a rational (and, metaphorically, a bloodless) utopia. It contains details taken from Plato, as well as from More; both men proposed such societies as methods of curing people's vices. Swift demonstrates, however, that these utopias are only suitable to fully rational and totally innocent creatures; they are only inhabitable by the type of creature who doesn't need the cure.

The rest of Book IV is spent exploring Gulliver's pride—the extraordinary and perverted pride that makes him aspire to be a horse.

Glossary

the sentiments of Socrates as Plato delivers them Socrates (470–399 B.C.) was an Athenian philosopher and teacher of Plato (427–347 B.C.), the Greek philosopher whose writings often feature Socrates in philosophical dialogues.

Chapter 9

Summary

Gulliver's master attends one of the Houyhnhnm assemblies, and, when he returns, he relates to Gulliver what happened. One horse, he says, contended that the filthy and vicious Yahoos should be exterminated because they are not native to the Country of the Houyhnhnms, they are instinctively hated, and they have been allowed to increase because they can be used as beasts of burden. It would be better if the Houyhnhnms had bred the useful, sweet-smelling, and hard-working donkey. Gulliver's master advanced an argument at the assembly that he borrowed from Gulliver: If Yahoos in England castrate Houyhnhnms, why couldn't the Houyhnhnms castrate the Yahoos?

Then Gulliver tells us more about the Houyhnhnms: They are a reasonable and healthy race. They understand the nature of the eclipse (the sum of their astronomy). They use only months to reckon time. They have no literature but do compose poetry which is moral and accurate. Their only word for evil is *Yahoo*. As for their houses, they build crude but clean and useful buildings. They use their hollow hooves as we use fingers and, considering this, are most adept. When Houyhnhnms die, they are buried quietly; there are no rituals and there is no mourning.

Commentary

Character Insight

In this chapter, Swift continues his thematic assault on humanity as represented by the Yahoos. The most obvious example relates to the general assembly's debate over the status of the Yahoos. The arguments for exterminating the Yahoos are compelling: The Yahoos are "the most filthy, noisome, and deformed animals which nature ever produced . . ." and they are "restive and indocible, mischievous and malicious." In terms of their evolution, the words used to describe the Yahoos are "degenerating by degrees." Not only this, but Gulliver tells the reader that the only reason that the Yahoos were eventually rounded up into herds was because the Houyhnhnms had "neglected to cultivate the breed of asses [donkeys and burros]" needed to do pulling and other basic labor tasks required in the Houyhnhnm society. In short, Yahoos are unnatural beasts and are hated by every other animal. Swift takes a slash at the philosophers of progress by suggesting that the Yahoos are simply a little further on the road to degeneration than are Europeans.

Character Insight

Gulliver cannot stand the Yahoos; he even suggests a method for exterminating them. Yet remember that, except for a semblance of reason and some clothing, he is very much like a Yahoo—indeed, he *is* a Yahoo. Why does he act this way? He has a fierce—and pathetic—pride, and this pride has given him disgust for his own species. He cannot bear to look at, and accept, the most squalid side of human nature. The alien, uncharitable, coldly rational horses seem far better creatures to try to emulate.

Glossary

indocible (indocile) not easy to teach or discipline.

aborigines of the land aborigines are the first or earliest known inhabitants of a region; here, meaning that the Yahoos were not native to the land of the Houyhnhnms—they came from some other location.

frog of the foot a triangular, horny pad in the posterior half of the sole of a horse's hoof.

Chapter 10

Summary

Gulliver grows more and more used to the Houyhnhnm way of life. He has a small room of his own with two chairs. He makes clothing of animal skins and shoes of Yahoo skins. He often dines on bread and honey. The conversation he listens to with the Houyhnhnms' permission is decent, moderate, polite, and virtuous. All Yahoos—native and European—seem detestable alongside the Houyhnhnms, and as best he can, Gulliver begins imitating the Houyhnhnm walk, speech, and manners.

Gulliver's attempt to become a Houyhnhnm frightens a number of the horses. They reason that Gulliver is a Yahoo—despite his clothes, his bit of reason, and the rest of his niceties—and they fear that he may organize the other Yahoos and revolt. They advise Gulliver's master to either treat his strange pet Yahoo like a Yahoo or command him to swim back to his native land. Gulliver is thunderstruck; he would prefer death. But finally he resolves to sail to an island visible from the Houyhnhnm coast. This decided, he builds a boat with the help of the sorrel servant. He covers the boat with Yahoo hides and caulks it with Yahoo fat. Then it is time for him to depart. His last request is to be allowed to kneel and kiss the hoof of his master.

Commentary

Character Insight

The reader has already seen Gulliver's pride operate to some extent in the earlier books. Gulliver identified himself with the giants in Book II, for example. Now he identifies himself with the horses. Gulliver's identification of himself with the giants produced only ludicrous results. But, in this book, his attempt to identify himself with the horses is more critical. The horses are alien to Gulliver; graphically, in their physical contrasts, they are not at all similar to him. Yet Gulliver thinks of the Yahoos as alien and animal. He makes traps of Yahoo hair. He makes shoes of Yahoo skin. He covers his boat with Yahoo skin and calicos it with Yahoo fat. Separating himself from his naturally depraved cousins, the Yahoos, Gulliver also separates himself from the European Yahoos.

He is near to madness—because of pride. Swift warns us of this danger by using the phrase "devoted to destruction" when Gulliver is sent away by the Houyhnhnms. The phrase is theological, describing those with an excess of pride, who reject charity and humility.

When Gulliver says, "When I thought of my family, my friends, my countrymen or [the] human race in general, I considered them as they really were, Yahoos in shape and disposition, only a little more civilized . . . ," he is, in essence, rejecting the society (including wife and family) that has produced him. He seeks admittance into "the perfection of nature," the society of the Houyhnhnms. Nevertheless, even though Gulliver recognizes several Houyhnhnm maxims, including, "*That nature is very easily satisfied*" and "*That necessity is the mother of invention*," he does not recognize a third, implied maxim (a maxim understood by Houyhnhnms, but not by Gulliver): "Once a Yahoo, always a Yahoo."

Glossary

ticking strong, heavy cloth, often striped, used for casings of mattresses, pillows, etc.

springes snares consisting of a noose attached to something under tension, as a bent tree branch.

splenetics irritable or spiteful people; here, another group of people whom Gulliver can avoid while living in the land of the Houyhnhnms.

the natural pravity (depravity) of those animals the inherent corruption and wickedness, the basic nature, of the Yahoos.

copse a thicket of small trees or shrubs.

Chapter 11

Summary

Gulliver sails to a nearby island where he is attacked by naked savages and forced to flee in his canoe back into the sea. Having nowhere else to go, he returns to another part of that same island. Coincidentally, a passing Portuguese ship sends a longboat to the island for water, and the sailors discover Gulliver. Gulliver trembles in fear but speaks to the sailors in their own language, with neighing intonations. He is horrified to be a prisoner of the Yahoos. Yet the captain of the ship, Pedro de Mendez, is kind. Gulliver is returned to Lisbon where Pedro de Mendez does all that he can to make Gulliver comfortable. Eventually, Don Pedro convinces Gulliver to return to his home in England.

Gulliver is happily received by his family (for they think that he is dead), but the reunion is a disaster for Gulliver: He cannot bear the sight or smell of his Yahoo-like wife and children. It is only after some time that he can bear to eat with them. To restore his mind, he spends much time in the stable.

Commentary

In Chapter 10, Swift has shown us Gulliver's fierce pride separating him from the Yahoos. He now shows this pride separating Gulliver from his own kind of (European) Yahoo. The savages who shoot arrows at Gulliver are, morally, somewhere between the depraved Yahoos and Pedro de Mendez. Mendez is a good and charitable man. He is not a rationalist stoic or a Deist filled with theories about the exalted dignity and natural benevolence of human nature. Yet Gulliver has lost his ability to evaluate; he treats Mendez as though the captain were merely a Yahoo. Mendez is a true Christian and shows the Christian virtue of charity. But blind to common sense, Gulliver cannot believe that a Yahoo can show virtue.

Character Insight

Swift has now concluded his illustration on humans' basic nature. Gulliver could not make himself a horse. He is not innocent or rational. He is, by nature, a Yahoo. But, as a European Yahoo, Gulliver should use his driblet of reason to improve himself; instead, he uses his reason to magnify his worst vice: his pride. Gulliver's pride has swelled out of all proportion; he has "reasoned" himself into rejecting his species and his nature: Gulliver is virtually a madman. His attitudes when he arrives in London make him a source of derision, for Gulliver seeks to change his basic nature by thinking; reason becomes the sole guide of his life.

Glossary

naturally arched by the force of tempests the island had been shaped by the force of winds.

veracity habitual truthfulness; honesty.

Inquisition the general tribunal established in the thirteenth century by the Roman Catholic Church for the discovery and prevention of heresy and the punishment of heretics; here, meaning that Gulliver felt that if the society to which he was returning learned about where he had been and what he had seen and learned, then he would risk being treated like a heretic.

Lisbon the capital of Portugal.

accoutred outfitted; equipped.

recluse a person who lives a secluded, solitary life; the kind of life hoped for by Gulliver at this time.

Chapter 12

Summary

Gulliver swears that all he has related is truthful, and he wishes that all travelers were forced to take an oath to tell the exact and literal truth. He hopes that the example of the Houyhnhnms will do the public some good; he intends only to make people wiser and better. He apologizes for not claiming his discoveries in the name of England, but he is proud that no one can accuse him of alluding to English politics in his writings. On a personal level, Gulliver is now able to eat with his family. Sometimes, he says, he instructs them in virtue. Concluding, he confesses that he could be reconciled to the English Yahoos "if they would be content with those Vices and Follies only which Nature hath entitled them to . . . but when I behold a Lump of Deformity, and Diseases both in Body and Mind, smitten with *Pride,* it immediately breaks all the Measures of my patience."

Commentary

In this final chapter, Swift returns to his normal, ironic joking. Gulliver swears that he tells the truth, slashing at lying authors of other voyage books. He denies that he uses political allusions; of course, however, Swift has attacked the Whigs almost continuously in the first three books. To make the joke even clearer to his literate audience, Swift has Gulliver quote Sinon (Virgil, *Aeneid,* II, 79–80). Sinon declares that he is telling the truth; in context, he is lying wholeheartedly.

Character Insight

In a last view of Gulliver's home life, we watch Gulliver still trying to become a horse. The scene is ridiculous, as if it is Gulliver's final warning against pride. The book ends on a note of deep irony; Gulliver is a prime example of the very pride he condemns.

Glossary

battering the warrior's faces into mummy by terrible yerks smashing the enemy by using kicks to the head.

CHARACTER ANALYSES

Lemuel Gulliver 77

The Lilliputians 78

The Brobdingnagians 79

The Houyhnhnms 80

The Yahoos 81

Lemuel Gulliver

Gulliver is the undistinguished third of five sons of a man of very modest means. He is of good and solid—but unimaginative—English stock. Gulliver was born in Nottinghamshire, a sedate county without eccentricity. He attended Emmanuel College, a respected, but not dazzling, school. The neighborhoods that Gulliver lived in—Old Jury, Fetter Lane, and Wapping—are all lower-middle-class sections. He is, in short, Mr. British middle class of his time.

Gulliver is also, as might be expected, "gullible." He believes what he is told. He is an honest man, and he expects others to be honest. This expectation makes for humor—and also for irony. We can be sure that what Gulliver tells us will be accurate. And we can also be fairly sure that Gulliver does not always understand the meaning of what he sees. The result is a series of astonishingly detailed, dead-pan scenes. For example, when Gulliver awakens in Lilliput, he *gradually* discovers, moving from one exact detail to another, that he is a prisoner of men six inches tall.

In Book I, Gulliver's possesses moral superiority to the petty—and tiny—Lilliputians, who show themselves to be a petty, cruel, vengeful, and self-serving race. Morally and politically, Gulliver is their superior. Here, Swift, through Gulliver, makes clear that the normal person is concerned with honor, gratitude, common sense, and kindness. The representative person (a Lilliputian) is a midget, figuratively and literally, compared with a moral person (Gulliver).

In Brobdingnag (Book II), Gulliver is still an ordinary moral man, but the Brobdingnagians are moral *giant* men. Certainly they are not perfect, but their moral superiority is as great to Gulliver as is their physical size. In his loyalty to England, we see that Gulliver is, in deed, a very proud man and one who accepts the madness and malice of British politics and society as the natural and normal standard. For the first time, we see Gulliver as the hypocrite—he lies to the Brobdingnagian king in order to conceal what is despicable about his native England. Gulliver's moral height can never reach that of the Brobdingnagians. Swift reinforces the idea of the giant's moral superiority by having Gulliver identify the English with the Lilliputians. This association also makes Gulliver ridiculous. It demonstrates the folly and self-deception that Gulliver practices in identifying himself with the moral giants. Gulliver's pride is at the root of his trouble. Swift dramatizes this with the mirror Gulliver cannot bear to look into.

In Book IV, Gulliver represents the middle ground between pure reason (as embodied by the Houyhnhnms) and pure animalism (as embodied by the depraved Yahoos), yet Gulliver's pride refuses to allow him to recognize the Yahoo aspects in himself. Therefore, he identifies himself with the Houyhnhnms and, in fact, tries to become one. But the horses are alien to Gulliver; yet Gulliver thinks of the Yahoos as alien and animal. Separating himself from his naturally depraved cousins, the Yahoos, Gulliver also separates himself from the European Yahoos. He is near to madness—because of pride. Gulliver has "reasoned" himself into rejecting his species and his nature: Gulliver is virtually a madman. His attitudes when he arrives in London make him a source of derision, for Gulliver seeks to change his basic nature by thinking; reason becomes the sole guide of his life.

In the end, Gulliver is still trying to acclimate himself to life as—and among—the Yahoos. Concluding, he confesses that he could be reconciled to the English Yahoos "if they would be content with those Vices and Follies only which Nature hath entitled them to. I am not in the least provoked at the sight of a Lawyer, a Pick-pocket, a Colonel, a Fool, a Lord, a Gamster, a Politician, a Whoremunger, a Physician, . . . or the like: This is all according to the due Course of Things: but, when I behold a Lump of Deformity, and Diseases both in Body and Mind, smitten with *Pride,* it immediately breaks all the Measures of my patience."

The Lilliputians

The Lilliputians are men six inches in height but possessing all the pretension and self-importance of full-sized men. They are mean and nasty, vicious, morally corrupt, hypocritical and deceitful, jealous and envious, filled with greed and ingratitude—they are, in fact, completely human.

Swift uses the Lilliputians to satirize specific events and people in his life. For example, Swift's model for Flimnap was Robert Walpole, the leader of the Whigs and England's first prime minister in the modern sense. Walpole was an extremely wily politician, as Swift shows, by making Flimnap the most dexterous of the rope dancers. Reldresal, the second most dexterous of the rope dancers, probably represents either Viscount Townshend or Lord Carteret. Both were political allies of Walpole.

The articles that Gulliver signs to obtain his freedom relate the political life of Lilliput to the political life of England. The articles themselves parallel particular English codes and laws. Similarly, the absurd and complicated method by which Gulliver must swear to the articles (he must hold his right foot in his left hand and place the middle finger of his right hand on top of his head with the right thumb on the tip of his ear) exemplifies an aspect of Whig politics: petty, red-tape harassing.

Swift also uses the Lilliputians to show that English politicians were bloody-minded and treacherous. In detail, he records the bloody and cruel methods that the Lilliputians plan to use to kill Gulliver; then he comments ironically on the mercy, decency, generosity, and justice of kings. The Lilliputian emperor, out of mercy, plans to blind and starve Gulliver—a direct reference to George's treatment of captured Jacobites, whom he executed—after parliament had called him most merciful and lenient.

By the end of Book I, Swift has drawn a brilliant, concrete, and detailed contrast between the normal, if gullible, man (Gulliver) and the diminutive but vicious politician (the Lilliputian); the politician is always a midget alongside Gulliver.

The Brobdingnagians

The Brobdingnagians are the epitome of moral giants. Physically huge—60 feet tall—their moral stature is also gigantic. Brobdingnag is a practical, moral utopia. Among the Brobdingnagians, there is good-will and calm virtue. Their laws encourage charity. Yet they are, underneath, just men who labor under every disadvantage to which man is heir. They are physically ugly when magnified, but they are morally beautiful. We cannot reject them simply because Gulliver describes them as physically gross. If we reject them, we become even more conscious of an ordinary person's verminous morality.

Set against the moral background of Brobdingnag and in comparison to the Brobdingnagians, Gulliver's "ordinariness" exposes many of its faults. Gulliver is revealed to be a very proud man and one who accepts the madness and malice of European politics, parties, and society as natural. What's more, he even lies to conceal what is despicable about them. The Brobdingnagian king, however, is not fooled by Gulliver. The English, he says, are "odious vermin."

Nevertheless, the Brobdingnagians are not without their flaws. Unlike Gulliver, who always considered the Lilliputians to be miniature men, the Brobdingnagians cannot think of Gulliver as a miniature Brobdingnagian. Even the King, who is sincerely fond of Gulliver, cannot view him as anything except an entertaining, albeit sly little fellow, one who is not to be trusted. The maids of honor in the Brobdingnagian court treat Gulliver as a plaything. To them, he is a toy, not a man, so they undress in front of him without a thought of modesty, and they titillate themselves with his naked body. Still, this "abuse" of Gulliver—denying his humanity and his *man*-hood—is done for amusement, not out of malice. Although they are not perfect, the Brobdingnagians are consistently moral. Only children and the deformed are intentionally evil.

In short, Swift praises the Brobdingnagians, but he does not intend for us to think that they are perfect humans. They are superhumans, bound to us by flesh and blood, just bigger morally than we are. Their virtues are not impossible for us to attain, but because it takes so much maturing to reach the stature of a moral giant, few humans achieve it.

The Houyhnhnms

Gulliver's description of the horses, the Houyhnhnms, is almost idyllic: "The behaviour of these animals was . . . orderly and rational . . . acute and judicious." Indeed, it is a horse that rescues him from the Yahoos—not by any overt, physical action, but by simply appearing on the road—no physical action being necessary.

Houyhnhnms live simple lives wholly devoted to reason. They speak clearly, they act justly, and they have simple laws. Each Houyhnhnm knows what is right and acts accordingly. They are untroubled by greed, politics, or lust. They live a life of cleanliness and exist in peace and serenity. They live by the grand maxim: Cultivate Reason and be totally governed by it. So perfect is their society, in fact, that they have no concept of a lie, and therefore no word to express it. The only word for evil is "Yahoo."

Swift defines *Houyhnhnm* as meaning "perfection of nature." This definition establishes an important distinction. The horses are uncorrupted by passion—either base or noble. They are devoid, for example, of charity. Also, they are not subject to temptation. Swift, however, never suggests that the Houyhnhnms stand for perfected human nature; on the contrary, they manifest *innocent* human nature. What they do—and what they say and think—*is* akin to human nature, but the character of the Houyhnhnms is far from Gulliver's. They are ignorant of many things which most people would consider venial. They cannot, for example, understand lying—or even the necessity for lying.

Swift thus establishes a range, or spectrum, of existence. The horses are literally innocent, having never (in theological terms) "fallen"; the Yahoos are super-sensual and seem depraved. The Houyhnhnms are ice-cold reason; the Yahoos are fiery sensuality. In between these extremes is Gulliver.

The Yahoos

Yahoos are the human-like creatures that Gulliver first encounters in the Country of the Houyhnhnms. Not recognizing their link with humanity, Gulliver describes the Yahoos as animals: ". . . deformed . . . . Their heads and breasts were covered with thick hair . . . but the rest of their bodies were bare . . .. They had no tails and often stood on their hind feet . . . ." He concludes with, "I never beheld in all my travels so disagreeable an animal."

Although they are human in form and feature, the Yahoos are, indeed, animals. They are filthy and they stink. They are omnivorous but seem to prefer meat and garbage. (Significantly, they eat nearly everything prohibited by the biblical and Levitical food codes.) They are "the most filthy, noisome, and deformed animals which nature ever produced . . ." and they are "restive and indocible, mischievous and malicious."

The Yahoos, however, are not merely animals; they are animals who are naturally vicious and represent Mankind depraved. Swift describes them in deliberately filthy and disgusting terms, often using metaphors drawn from dung. In terms of their evolution, the words used to describe the Yahoos are "degenerating by degrees."

Swift positions Gulliver midway—figuratively and literally—between the super-rational, innocent horses (the Houyhnhnms) and the filthy, depraved Yahoos. Gulliver, however, reacts to the Yahoos with immediate and overpowering detestation and is horrified by the Yahoos' similarity to him. He lacks the humility to see himself as a sort of Yahoo. Rather, his pride leads him to try to become a horse. Gulliver will try with admirable determination to improve himself; he will try to change himself into a more horse-like state, but he will fail. He is, simply, more of a Yahoo than a Houyhnhnm.

CRITICAL ESSAYS

Philosophical and Political Background 83

Swift's Satire 88

Gulliver as a Dramatis Persona 90

Philosophical and Political Background

Swift has at least two aims in *Gulliver's Travels* besides merely telling a good adventure story. Behind the disguise of his narrative, he is satirizing the pettiness of human nature in general and attacking the Whigs in particular. By emphasizing the six-inch height of the Lilliputians, he graphically diminishes the stature of politicians and indeed the stature of all human nature. And in using the fire in the Queen's chambers, the rope dancers, the bill of particulars drawn against Gulliver, and the inventory of Gulliver's pockets, he presents a series of allusions that were identifiable to his contemporaries as critical of Whig politics.

Why, one might ask, did Swift have such a consuming contempt for the Whigs? This hatred began when Swift entered politics as the representative of the Irish church. Representing the Irish bishops, Swift tried to get Queen Anne and the Whigs to grant some financial aid to the Irish church. They refused, and Swift turned against them even though he had considered them his friends and had helped them while he worked for Sir William Temple. Swift turned to the Tories for political allegiance and devoted his propaganda talents to their services. Using certain political events of 1714–18, he described in *Gulliver's Travels* many things that would remind his readers that Lilliputian folly was also English folly—and, particularly, Whig folly. The method, for example, which Gulliver must use to swear his allegiance to the Lilliputian emperor parallels the absurd difficulty that the Whigs created concerning the credentials of the Tory ambassadors who signed the Treaty of Utrecht.

Swift's craftiness was successful. His book was popular because it was a compelling adventure tale and also a puzzle. His readers were eager to identify the various characters and discuss their discoveries, and, as a result, many of them saw politics and politicians from a new perspective.

Within the broad scheme *of Gulliver's Travels*, Gulliver seems to be an average man in eighteenth-century England. He is concerned with family and with his job, yet he is confronted by the pigmies that politics and political theorizing make of people. Gulliver is utterly incapable of the stupidity of the Lilliputian politicians, and, therefore, he and the Lilliputians are ever-present contrasts for us. We are always aware of the difference between the imperfect (but normal) moral life of Gulliver, and the petty and stupid political life of emperors, prime ministers, and informers.

In the second book of the *Travels*, Swift reverses the size relationship that he used in Book I. In Lilliput, Gulliver was a giant; in Brobdingnag, Gulliver is a midget. Swift uses this difference to express a difference in morality. Gulliver was an ordinary man compared to the amoral political midgets in Lilliput. Now, Gulliver remains an ordinary man, but the Brobdingnagians are *moral* men. They are not perfect, but they are consistently moral. Only children and the deformed are intentionally evil.

Set against a moral background, Gulliver's "ordinariness" exposes many of its faults. Gulliver is revealed to be a very proud man and one who accepts the madness and malice of European politics, parties, and society as natural. What's more, he even lies to conceal what is despicable about them. The Brobdingnagian king, however, is not fooled by Gulliver. The English, he says, are "odious vermin."

Swift praises the Brobdingnagians, but he does not intend for us to think that they are perfect humans. They are superhumans, bound to us by flesh and blood, just bigger morally than we are. Their virtues are not impossible for us to attain, but because it takes so much maturing to reach the stature of a moral giant, few humans achieve it.

Brobdingnag is a practical, moral utopia. Among the Brobdingnagians, there is goodwill and calm virtue. Their laws encourage charity. Yet they are, underneath, just men who labor under every disadvantage to which man is heir. They are physically ugly when magnified, but they are morally beautiful. We cannot reject them simply because Gulliver describes them as physically gross. If we reject them, we become even more conscious of an ordinary person's verminous morality.

In Books I and II, Swift directs his satire more toward individual targets than firing broadside at abstract concepts. In Book I, he is primarily concerned with Whig politics and politicians rather than with the abstract politician; in Book II, he elects to reprove immoral Englishmen rather than abstract immorality. In Book III, Swift's target is somewhat abstract—pride in reason—but he also singles out and censures a group of his contemporaries whom he believed to be particularly depraved in their exaltation of reason. He attacks his old enemies, the Moderns, and their satellites, the Deists and rationalists. In opposition to their credos, Swift believed that people were capable of reasoning, but that they were far from being fully rational. For the record, it should probably be mentioned that Swift was not alone in denouncing this clique of people. The objects of Swift's indignation had also aroused the rage of Pope, Arbuthnot, Dryden, and most of the orthodox theologians of the Augustan Age.

This love of reason that Swift criticizes derived from the rationalism of the seventeenth and eighteenth centuries. John Locke's theories of natural religion were popularly read, as were Descartes' theories about the use of reason. Then a loosely connected group summarized these opinions, plus others, and a cult was born: They called themselves the Deists.

In general, the Deists believed that people could reason, observe the universe accurately, and perceive axioms intuitively. With these faculties, people could then arrive at religious truth; they did not need biblical revelation. Orthodox theology has always made reason dependent on God and morality, but the Deists refuted this notion. They attacked revealed religion, saying that if reason can support the God described by the Bible, it may also conclude that God is quite different from the biblical God. The answer depends upon which observations and axioms the reasoner chooses to use.

Even before he wrote the *Travels*, Swift opposed excessive pride in reason. In his ironical *Argument Against Abolishing Christianity*, he makes plain what he considers to be the consequences of depending on reason, rather than upon faith and revelation. Disbelief, he said, is the consequence of presumptuous pride in reasoning, and immorality is the consequence of disbelief. Swift believed that religion holds moral society together. A person who does not believe in God by faith and revelation is in danger of disbelieving in morality.

To Swift, rationalism leads to Deism, Deism to atheism, and atheism to immorality. Where people worship reason, they abandon tradition and common sense. Both tradition and common sense tell humankind that murder, whoring, and drunkenness, for example, are immoral. Yet, if one depends on reason for morality, that person can find no proof that one should not drink, whore, or murder. Thus, reasonably, is one not free to do these things? Swift believed that will, rather than reason, was far too often the master.

Alexander Pope agreed with the position that Swift took. In his *Essay on Man*, he states that people cannot perceive accurately. Our axioms are usually contradictory, and our rational systems of living in a society are meaninglessly abstract. People, he insists, are thoroughly filled with self-love and pride; they are incapable of being rational—that is, objective. Swift would certainly concur.

In Book III, Laputan systematizing is exaggerated, but Swift's point is clear and concrete: Such systematizing is a manifestation of proud rationalism. The Laputans think so abstractly that they have lost their hold on common sense. They are so absorbed in their abstractions that they serve food in geometric and musical shapes. Everything is relegated to abstract thought, and the result is mass delusion and chaos. The Laputans do not produce anything useful; their clothes do not fit, and their houses are not constructed correctly. These people think—but only for abstract thinking's sake; they do not consider ends.

In a similar fashion, Swift shows that philology and scholarship betray the best interests of the Luggnaggians; pragmatic scientism fails in Balnibarbi; and accumulated experience does not make the Struld-bruggs either happy or wise. In his topical political references, Swift demonstrates the viciousness and cruelty, as well as the folly, that arise from abstract political theory imposed by selfish politicians. The common people, Swift says, suffer. He also cites the folly of Laputan theorists and the Laputan king by referring to the immediate political blunders of the Georges.

The *Travels* is structured very much like a variation on the question, "Why are people so often vicious and cruel?" and the answer, "Because they succumb to the worst elements in themselves." Man is an infinitely complex animal; he is many, many mixtures of intellect and reason, charity and emotion. Yet reason and intellect are not synonymous—even if they might profitably be; nor are emotion and charity necessarily akin to one another. But few people see Man as the grey mixture of varying qualities that he is. Man oversimplifies, and, in the last book of the *Travels*, Swift shows us the folly of people who advance such theories. In his time, it was a popular notion that a Reasonable Man was a Complete Man. Here, Swift shows us Reason exalted. We must judge whether it is possible or desirable for Man.

The Houyhnhnms are super-reasonable. They have all the virtues that the stoics and Deists advocated. They speak clearly, they act justly, and they have simple laws. They do not quarrel or argue since each knows what is true and right. They do not suffer from the uncertainties of reasoning that afflict Man. But they are so reasonable that they have no emotions. They are untroubled by greed, politics, or lust. They act from undifferentiated benevolence. They would never prefer the welfare of one of their own children to the welfare of another Houyhnhnm simply on the basis of kinship.

Very simply, the Houyhnhnms *are* horses; they are *not* humans. And this physical difference parallels the abstract difference. They are fully rational, innocent, and undepraved. Man is capable of reason, but never wholly or continuously, and he is—but never wholly or continuously— passionate, proud, and depraved.

In contrast to the Houyhnhnms, Swift presents their precise opposite: the Yahoos, creatures who exhibit the essence of sensual human sinfulness. The Yahoos are not merely animals; they are animals who are naturally vicious. Swift describes them in deliberately filthy and disgusting terms, often using metaphors drawn from dung. The Yahoos plainly represent Mankind depraved. Swift, in fact, describes the Yahoos in such disgusting terms that early critics assumed that he hated Man to the point of madness. Swift, however, takes his descriptions from the sermons and theological tracts of his predecessors and contemporaries. If Swift hated Man, one would also have to say that St. Francis and St. Augustine did, too. Swift's descriptions of depraved Man are, if anything, milder than they might be. One sermon writer described Man as a *saccus stercorum*, a sack filled with dung. The descriptions of the Yahoos do not document Swift's supposed misanthropy. Rather, the creatures exhibit physically the moral flaws and natural depravity that theologians say plague the offspring of Adam.

Midway between the poles of the Houyhnhnms and the Yahoos, Swift places Gulliver. Gulliver is an average man, except that he has become irrational in his regard for reason. Gulliver is so disgusted with the Yahoos and so admires the Houyhnhnms that he tries to become a horse.

This aspiration to become a horse exposes Gulliver's grave weakness. Gullible and proud, he becomes such a devotee of reason that he cannot accept his fellow humans who are less than totally reasonable. He cannot recognize virtue and charity when they exist. Captain Pedro de Mendez rescues Gulliver and takes him back to Europe, but Gulliver despises him because Mendez doesn't look like a horse. Likewise, when he reaches home, Gulliver hates his family because they look and smell like Yahoos. He is still capable of seeing objects and surfaces accurately, but he is incapable of grasping true depths of meaning.

Swift discriminates between people as they are idealized, people as they are damned, people as they possibly could be, and others as they are. The Houyhnhnms embody the ideal of the rationalists and stoics; the Yahoos illustrate the damning abstraction of sinful and depraved

Man; and Pedro de Mendez represents virtue possible to Man. Gulliver, usually quite sane, is misled when we leave him, but he is like most people. Even dullards, occasionally, become obsessed by something or other for a while before lapsing back into their quiet, workaday selves. Eventually, we can imagine that Gulliver will recover and be his former unexciting, gullible self.

Swift uses the technique of making abstractions concrete to show us that super-reasonable horses are impossible and useless models for humans. They have never fallen and therefore have never been redeemed. They are incapable of the Christian virtues that unite passion and reason: Neither they nor the Yahoos are touched by grace or charity. In contrast, the Christian virtues of Pedro de Mendez and the Brobdingnagians (the "least corrupted" of mankind) are possible to humans. These virtues are the result of grace and redemption. Swift does not press this theological point, however. He is, after all, writing a satire, not a religious tract.

Swift's Satire

Gulliver's Travels was unique in its day; it was not written to woo or entertain. It was an indictment, and it was most popular among those who were indicted—that is, politicians, scientists, philosophers, and Englishmen in general. Swift was roasting people, and they were eager for the banquet.

Swift himself admitted to wanting to "vex" the world with his satire, and it is certainly in his tone, more than anything else, that one most feels his intentions. Besides the coarse language and bawdy scenes, probably the most important element that Dr. Bowdler deleted from the original *Gulliver's Travels* was this satiric tone. The tone of the original varies from mild wit to outright derision, but always present is a certain strata of ridicule. Dr. Bowdler gelded it of its satire and transformed it into a children's book.

After that literary operation, the original version was largely lost to the common reader. The *Travels* that proper Victorians bought for the family library was Bowdler's version, not Swift's. What irony that Bowdler would have laundered the *Travels* in order to get a version that he believed to be best for public consumption because, originally, the book was bought so avidly by the public that booksellers were raising the price of the volume, sure of making a few extra shillings on this bestseller.

And not only did the educated buy and read the book—so also did the largely uneducated.

However, lest one think that Swift's satire is merely the weapon of exaggeration, it is important to note that exaggeration is only one facet of his satiric method. Swift uses mock seriousness and understatement; he parodies and burlesques; he presents a virtue and then turns it into a vice. He takes pot-shots at all sorts of sacred cows. Besides science, Swift debunks the whole sentimental attitude surrounding children. At birth, for instance, Lilliputian children were "wisely" taken from their parents and given to the State to rear. In an earlier satire (*A Modest Proposal*), he had proposed that the very poor in Ireland sell their children to the English as gourmet food.

Swift is also a name-caller. Mankind, as he has a Brobdingnagian remark, is "the most pernicious race of little odious vermin that Nature ever suffered to crawl upon the surface of the earth." Swift also inserted subtly hidden puns into some of his name-calling techniques. The island of Laputa, the island of pseudo-science, is literally (in Spanish) the land of "the whore." Science, which learned people of his generation were venerating as a goddess, Swift labeled a whore, and devoted a whole hook to illustrating the ridiculous behavior of her converts.

In addition, Swift mocks blind devotion. Gulliver, leaving the Houyhnhnms, says that he "took a second leave of my master, but as I was going to prostrate myself to kiss his hoof, he did me the honor to raise it gently to my mouth." Swift was indeed so thorough a satirist that many of his early readers misread the section on the Houyhnhnms. They were so enamored of reason that they did not realize that Swift was metamorphosing a virtue into a vice. In Book IV, Gulliver has come to idealize the horses. They embody pure reason, but they are not human. Literally, of course, we know they are not, but figuratively they seem an ideal for humans—until Swift exposes them as dull, unfeeling creatures, thoroughly unhuman. They take no pleasure in sex, nor do they ever overflow with either joy or melancholy. They are bloodless.

Gulliver's Travels was the work of a writer who had been using satire as his medium for over a quarter of a century. His life was one of continual disappointment, and satire was his complaint and his defense—against his enemies and against humankind. People, he believed, were generally ridiculous and petty, greedy and proud; they were blind to the "ideal of the mean." This ideal of the mean was present in one of Swift's first major satires, *The Battle of the Books* (1697). There, Swift took the side of the Ancients, but he showed their views to be ultimately as distorted as those of their adversaries, the Moderns. In Gulliver's last adventure, Swift again pointed to the ideal of the mean by positioning Gulliver between symbols of sterile reason and symbols of gross sensuality. To Swift, Man is a mixture of sense and nonsense; he had accomplished much but had fallen far short of what he could have been and what he could have done.

Swift was certainly not one of the optimists typical of his century. He did not believe that the Age of Science was the triumph that a great majority of his countrymen believed it to be. Science and reason needed limits, and they needed a good measure of humanism. They did not require absolute devotion.

Swift was a highly moral man and was shocked by his contemporaries' easy conversion to reason as the be-all and end-all of philosophy. To be so gullible amounted to non-reason in Swift's thinking. He therefore offered up the impractical scientists of Laputa and the impersonal, but absolutely reasonable, Houyhnhnms as embodiments of science and reason carried to ridiculous limits. Swift, in fact, created the whole of *Gulliver's Travels* in order to give the public a new moral lens. Through this lens, Swift hoped to "vex" his readers by offering them new insights into the game of politics and into the social follies of humans.

Gulliver as a Dramatis Persona

Jonathan Swift is not, of course, Lemuel Gulliver; nor does Swift seriously use Gulliver as either a mask or a mouthpiece. This truism, however, is not as obvious as one might think. For too many years, critics of *Gulliver's Travels* were infuriated with Swift. After they had finished the fourth book of the *Travels*, they believed that Swift had imbued Gulliver with his own mad and misanthropic traits. Thackeray, for instance, said that Swift should be "hooted" because he had written a book "filthy in word, filthy in thought . . . raging [and] obscene." Swift's early critics were quick to forget—or carelessly overlooked in their horror—that Gulliver's denunciation of the Yahoos and his veneration for the Houyhnhnms belonged to *Gulliver*—a character in an allegorical adventure tale. He was Swift's creation, but never the creator himself.

Gulliver is a simple, naive creature; Swift is one of the most complex personalities in English letters. Swift merely incensed his early critics, and they wanted a scapegoat on which to vent their ire. The same critics would not have dreamed of identifying Swift with Gulliver while Gulliver was amongst the Lilliputians, but when Swift placed Gulliver between the extremes of the Yahoos and the Houyhnhnms, then the satire became less topical. Swift, in the fourth book, is assailing Man, not merely English, political men. But it is not Swift who is saying that all humankind is worthless; it is Gulliver who thought so. Swift set up the antithetical worlds of the Yahoos and the Houyhnhnms to shock, not to define. Gulliver, if properly viewed, is a fool when the *Travels* is finished. He prefers the company of horses to other men and even to his own family. Ironically, he worships reason but is almost wholly devoid of reason.

The kind of a man Swift was and the kind of a man Gulliver is are antithetical to one another. Gulliver is an "innocent-eyed" narrator; Swift was an ironist. Gulliver tells us what he believes is the truth; Swift reveals ambiguities. Gulliver reports to us as precisely as he can, often not realizing the implications of his observations. Swift, in contrast, lets us know the implications. Gulliver, for example, is impressed by the Lilliputians' grandeur; Swift lets us see beyond Gulliver's narrative line and realize the irony in the juxtaposition of the miniscule Lilliputians and their grandiose notions. Gulliver gives us his perspective of his adventures; then Swift pulls us farther back so that Gulliver himself is seen in perspective. Yet one thing that we can always count on, as far as Gulliver is concerned, is his honesty as a reporter. We can trust him because he is neither discreet nor imaginative enough to either withhold or insert inventive adventures on his own.

The tone that Swift has Gulliver use in reporting is one of the key factors separating author from hero. Gulliver reports to us as though we were as gullible as he is. Of course we are not. We can feel superior to Gulliver even though we like him. He has a fascinating curiosity and gets himself into many scrapes precisely because of his gullibility. Had he been as clever as Swift, there would have been no adventures. In fact, Swift would probably have so infuriated the Brobdingnagians that they would have snuffed out his life. They would not have tolerated the stinging-tongued little Dean.

One may argue that ultimately Gulliver is disillusioned about man, and so is Swift. But Swift was never so disillusioned about people that he boarded in a stable. Swift's disillusionment took an indignant turn. That's why he wrote his satires—to point out imperfections, to chasten, and to educate. Swift was his own judge. But Gulliver accepts the

Houyhnhnms' judgment of himself. And he finally believes that he, though he hates to admit it, is terribly Yahoo-like. Gulliver worships the Houyhnhnm ideal; Swift subtly mocks it by letting Gulliver praise it; then he slowly reveals that it is an ideal devoid of any spark of life. In this way, Swift shows us that Gulliver is incapable of critically thinking and reasoning. Gulliver is worshipping something as lifeless as a mathematical equation. And, when we finish the book, the horses and their ideals are as uninteresting to us as they are captivating to Gulliver.

Gulliver is completely befuddled at the end of the *Travels*. He has reached for an unhuman ideal and has rejected the sub-human Yahoos as too thoroughly human. He believes that the *Travels* is a defense of himself, showing how morally he acted. In truth, the *Travels* is the best evidence one could have that Gulliver often acted very ridiculously. He imagines one type of audience; Swift created for another. Gulliver's gullibility and his simplicity are responsible for his downfall. He does not realize that human beings are infinitely more complex than the Yahoos or the Houyhnhnms. Being a simple man, he simplifies to disastrous extremes. He has come full turn—from being proud of being a European man to disgust for all people. Gulliver believes his distorted vision. Swift does not. He holds it up only as a disconcerting, shocking mirror image—the kind one finds at a carnival. This is the reason for his satire—to catch us off-guard, to magnify, to miniaturize, and to make us *see* anew.

CliffsNotes Review

Use this CliffsNotes Review to test your understanding of the original text and reinforce what you've learned in this book. After you work through the review and essay questions, identify the quote section, and the fun and useful practice projects, you're well on your way to understanding a comprehensive and meaningful interpretation of *Gulliver's Travels*.

Q&A

1. *Gulliver's Travels* is essentially a satire on

- **a.** rulers' abuses of their subjects
- **b.** the problems of dysfunctional families
- **c.** the nature of man

2. In the utopia called the Country of the Houyhnhnms, the horses represent

- **a.** dominance by force
- **b.** "the perfection of nature"
- **c.** the entanglements of power

3. Throughout the *Travels*, we recognize that Gulliver's greatest fault is his

- **a.** pride
- **b.** loyalty
- **c.** gullibility

4. Swift's satiric treatment of the academies of Balnibarbi focuses on the experiments, called

- **a.** grants
- **b.** studies
- **c.** projects

5. Gulliver's visit to Lilliput allows Swift to satirize rulers who have

- **a.** small views and narrow interests
- **b.** big ideas and grandiose plans
- **c.** preoccupations with specific topics

6. In Brobdingnag, the only immoral or malicious people are

a. greedy farmers

b. the deformed and children

c. members of the royal court

Answers: (1) c. (2) b. (3) a. (4) c. (5) a. (6) b.

Identify the Quote

1. When I thought of my family, my friends, my countrymen, or human race in general I considered them as they really were, Yahoos in shape and disposition . . . .

2. I cannot but conclude the bulk of your natives to be the most pernicious race of little odious vermin that nature ever suffered to crawl upon the surface of the earth.

Answers: (1) [Gulliver is making an observation about all of humanity after experiencing living with the Houyhnhnms and the Yahoos and having been on four voyages to various lands.] (2) [The King of Brobdingnag shares his assessment of humankind with Gulliver.]

Essay Questions

1. Some would argue that Swift was a misanthrope and that *Gulliver's Travels* proves his hatred of mankind. Agree or disagree with this assessment and support your opinion with examples from the text.

2. Explain how Swift makes use of the character of Gulliver. As you prepare your answer, be sure to consider whether Gulliver has a distinct and recognizable character or whether he is simply Swift's mouthpiece.

3. In his satire, Swift makes a correlation between size and morality. Explain how this works in the *Travels*, paying particular attention to Gulliver in Lilliput and in Brobdingnag.

Practice Projects

1. Identify specific characters satirized in *Gulliver's Travels* and determine the actual historical figures whom Swift had in mind for his satire.

2. View any of the film versions of *Gulliver's Travels* (see the Resources section for information) and note differences in plot, settings, characterizations, and theme (satiric treatments) between the film and the novel.

3. Identify the most serious behavior flaws of the Yahoos, and design a program of rehabilitation for the Yahoos. List the specific behaviors to be corrected and the specific remedies, whether physical, occupational, recreational, or medical, which would be required.

4. Identify and explain the evidence which could be used to identify Gulliver as a Yahoo, as well as the evidence which could indicate that he is not a Yahoo. Using this evidence, support or overturn the general assembly's decision to expel Gulliver from the Country of the Houyhnhnms.

CliffsNotes Resource Center

The learning doesn't need to stop here. CliffsNotes Resource Center shows you the best of the best—links to the best information in print and online about the author and/or related works. And don't think that this is all we've prepared for you; we've put all kinds of pertinent information at www.cliffsnotes.com. Look for all the terrific resources at your favorite bookstore or local library and on the Internet. When you're online, make your first stop www.cliffsnotes.com where you'll find more incredibly useful information about *Gulliver's Travels*.

Books

This CliffsNotes book provides a meaningful interpretation of *Gulliver's Travels*. If you are looking for information about the author and/or related works, check out these other publications:

The Oxford Illustrated History of the British Monarchy, by John Cannon and Ralph Griffiths. Over 400 illustrations help readers discover the stories and cultural milieu of British monarchs—from Anglo-Saxon times to the present. New York: Oxford University Press, 1988.

Jonathan Swift: A Portrait, by Victoria Glendinning, is a biography of Swift that examines his political and artistic perspectives and explores the satirist's romantic relationships as well. New York: Holt, 1999.

The Pleasures of the Imagination: English Culture in the Eighteenth Century, by John Brewer, focuses on eighteenth-century arts, including a social history of the artistic forces at play during Swift's mature years. Chicago: University of Chicago Press, 2000.

Imagining Monsters: Miscreations of the Self in Eighteenth-Century England, by Dennis Todd, addresses Swift's and his contemporaries' ideas about the roles of the imagination and self identity in life and art. Chicago: University of Chicago Press, 1995.

It's easy to find books published by IDG Books Worldwide, Inc. You'll find them in your favorite bookstores (on the Internet and at a store near you). We also have three Web sites that you can use to read about all the books we publish:

- www.cliffsnotes.com
- www.dummies.com
- www.idgbooks.com

Internet

Check out these Web resources for more information about Jonathan Swift and *Gulliver's Travels*:

Gulliver's Travels by Jonathan Swift, www.jaffebros.com/lee/gulliver/—Created by Lee Jaffe and hosted by the Jaffe brothers, this site provides information on bibliographies, dictionary terms, quotations, timelines, and other items related to *Gulliver's Travels*.

Gulliver's Travels, litrix.com/gulliver/gulli001.htm—This site contains the complete text of Gulliver's Travels, which you can access by chapter and book.

The Marvels of Swift, www.geocities.com/SoHo/Nook/7255/—This site contains links to complete texts of several of Swift's works, including *Gulliver's Travels*. Note, however, that it does not include some of his major publications, such as the *Drapier Papers* or *Tale of the Tub*.

The Jonathan Swift Page, www.accd.edu/sac/english/bailey/swift.htm—This site includes a photo and links to several works written by Swift. Biographical references are also listed.

Next time you're on the Internet, don't forget to drop by www.cliffsnotes.com. We created an online Resource Center that you can use today, tomorrow, and beyond.

Films and Other Recordings

Following are recordings and films that may aid you in your study of Jonathan Swift and *Gulliver's Travels*:

Gulliver's Travels, Paramount, 1939. This animated film version of *Gulliver's Travels*, which features the voice talent of Sam Parker, Lanny Ross, and others, focuses only on Gulliver's voyage to Lilliput.

Gulliver's Travels, Sunn Classics, 1977. Directed by Peter Hunt and featuring Richard Harris and Catherine Schell, this movie is classified in the genre of fantasy and includes several animators on the production staff.

Gulliver's Travels, Hallmark Home Entertainment, 1996. Directed by Charles Sturridge and starring Ted Danson and Mary Steenburgen, this video, originally a made-for-television miniseries, includes references to all of Gulliver's voyages.

Gulliver's Travels. Blackstone Audio, 1986. Read by Walter Covell, this is an unabridged reading of *Gulliver's Travels* and includes eight tapes.

Magazines and Journals

For more information about *Gulliver's Travels*, you may want to refer to the following articles:

Donoghue, Denis. "The Brainwashing of Lemuel Gulliver." *Southern Review* 32 (1996): 128–146. An interesting article that addresses the effects Gulliver's travels had on him mentally.

Richardson, John. "Still to Seek: Politics, Irony, Swift." *Essays in Criticism* 49 (1999): 300–319. A helpful article that discusses the political (and power) influences on Swift's writings.

Send Us Your Favorite Tips

In your quest for knowledge, have you ever experienced that sublime moment when you figure out a trick that saves time or trouble? Perhaps you realized you were taking ten steps to accomplish something that could have taken two. Or you found a little-known workaround that achieved great results. If you've discovered a useful resource that gave you insight into or helped you understand *Gulliver's Travels* and you'd like to share it, the CliffsNotes staff would love to hear from you. Go to our Web site at www.cliffsnotes.com and click the Talk to Us button. If we select your tip, we may publish it as part of CliffsNotes Daily, our exciting, free e-mail newsletter. To find out more or to subscribe to a newsletter, go to on the Web.

Index

A

abstractions made concrete, 5, 53, 88
Academy Projectors (Professors), 8, 47
Adventure (ship), 27
Aeneid (Virgil), 75
Amboyna (ship), 55
Ancients, 3, 90
animalism versus reason, 78
Anne, Queen, 20, 83
Antelope (ship), 11
Arbuthnot, John, 85
Argument Against Abolishing Christianity
  (Swift), 3, 85
Aristotle, 51
astrology, 43, 44
astronomy, 45, 69
Atterbury, Bishop, 22, 49

B

Balnibarbi
  described, 47
  engineering mentality, effect of, 47
  Laputan tyranny over, 45
  political scientists, 49
  projects, 47, 48, 93
  taxation, 49
Bath, Order of the, 15
Battle of the Books (Swift), 39, 89
Berkley, Lord, 2
Big Endians, 17, 18
Blefuscu, 17, 19, 23, 25
Boleyn, Anne, 18
Bolingbroke, Henry Saint John, 13, 19, 23,
  25
Bowdler, Dr. Thomas, 88
"Brainwashing of Lemuel Gulliver, The"
  (Donoghue), 98
Brobdingnag
  England compared, 33
  government, 38
  laws, 38, 39
  utopian, 79, 84

Brobdingnagian king
  England, opinion of, 31, 37
  humans, opinion of, 32, 37
  "pernicious race of little odious vermin"
    quote, 37, 89, 94
Brobdingnagian queen, 31
Brobdingnagians
  beggars, 33
  children, 29, 94
  deformed, 29, 94
  the dwarf, 31, 34
  Gulliver, opinion of, 27, 31, 34, 80
  Gulliver, treatment of, 29, 34, 80
  illnesses, 33
  Lilliputians compared, 27
  moral virtue of, 28, 29, 77, 79, 84
  repulsiveness of, 28, 79
  as superhuman, 84

C

Cannon, John, 96
Carteret, Lord, 16, 78
Charles I, 11, 18
children, 21, 29, 89
Church of Ireland, Swift's career with, 2, 20,
  83
clothing, 43, 59, 62. *See also* nakedness
Conduct of the Allies, The (Swift), 41
crucifix-trampling ceremony, 55

D

de Mendez, Pedro, 73, 87, 88
dead brought back, 50, 51
Deism, 84, 85. See also reason
Descartes, 51, 85
Didymus Chalcenterus, 51
diet. See food
Dingley, Rebecca, 3
Dionysius of Halicarnassus, 39
disease, 33, 51, 65
doctors, 65
Drapier's Letters, The (Swift), 3, 46
Dryden, John, 85
Dublin, 46
Dublin University, 2
Duns Scotus, John, 51
Dutch language, 60
Dutch, the, 41, 53, 55

E

egg-breaking question, 17
England
    Brobdingnag compared, 33
    Brobdingnagian king's opinion of, 37
    France wars with, 17, 19
    Gulliver idealizes, 36, 38
    Gulliver's loyalty to, 77
    Ireland, relation to, 3, 45
    Lilliput as, 16, 40, 77, 78, 83
    politicians, comments on, 23, 79
English, the
    Brobdingnagian king's opinion
        of, 31
    degenerated from rich diet and
        syphilis, 51
    as Yahoos, 64, 75, 78
Essay on Man (Pope), 85
Eustanthius, 51
excrement
    food, reconverting to, 48
    treason discerned by reading, 49
    Yahoo association with, 87
    Yahoos defecate on Gulliver, 56, 57
experience as best teacher, 54

F

Fable of the Bees (Mandeville), 65
faith, 43
Flimnap
    Gulliver, slanders, 19, 21
    rope dancing abilities, 15
    Walpole model for, 15, 78
floor licking, 53
Flying Island, 41, 45
flying island device in satire, 41
food
    excrement, restoring from, 48
    gourmet, 65, 89
    Gulliver in Houyhnhnmland, 58, 59
    Gulliver in Lilliput, 15
    Houyhnhnms, 58
    Irish children as, 89
    Laputan, 86
    vice/diet analogy, 65
    Yahoos, 58
France, 17, 19

G

Garter, Order of the, 15
Gassendi, Pierre, 51
George I
    appearance, 13
    German origin, 29, 44
    Jacobites, treatment of, 23, 79
    Lilliputian emperor compared, 13
    political support, buying, 15
George II, 18
Glubbdubdrib, 50
Glumdalclitch, 29, 31
Grand Academy, 48
Grey Horse, 8, 58
Griffiths, Ralph, 96
Gulliver
    background, 11, 77
    Brobdingnagians opinion of, 27, 31,
        34, 80
    Brobdingnagians treatment of, 29, 34, 80
    England, idealizes, 36, 38
    gullibility, 11, 32, 77, 91, 93
    horse, wishes to become, 59, 71, 87
    Houyhnhnms, compared to, 81
    Houyhnhnms, identifies with, 78
    Houyhnhnms, midway between Yahoos
        and, 58, 59, 61, 87
    hypocrisy of, 77
    immortality, envies, 54
    introduced, 7
    Lilliputian emperor, pact with, 15, 16
    Lilliputian treason accusations, 23
    Lilliputians, respect for, 13
    loyalty, 77, 93
    mirror, unable to look into, 40
    modesty, 60
    moral virtue of, 11, 16, 25, 77
    ordinariness of, 11, 77, 83, 84
    pride, 38, 74, 93
    pride causes disgust with humanity, 70,
        73, 81
    pride, condemns, 75
    pride drives to madness, 72, 78
    pride identifies with moral giants, 40
    pride in Europe, 84
    pride over sword abilities, 34
    reason, adopts as guide, 78
    Swift contrasted with, 90–92, 94
    "When I thought of my family" quote,
        72, 94

as Yahoo, 70, 74
Yahoo body parts, uses, 71
Yahoos, compared to, 81
Yahoos, revulsion to, 59
Yahoos, sees humanity as, 72, 73, 87
Yahoos, separates himself from, 78
Gulliver's Travels (animated film, 1939), 97
Gulliver's Travels (audio recording, 1986), 98
Gulliver's Travels (film, 1977), 98
Gulliver's Travels (video, 1996), 98
Gulliver's Travels by Jonathan Swift Web site, 97
Gulliver's Travels Web site, 97
gunpowder, 38, 39, 48

H

Harley, Robert, 13, 19, 23, 25
Henry VIII, 18
High Heel party, 8, 17, 18
historians, 50, 51
history, 50, 51
Homer, 51
Hopewell (ship), 41
Houyhnhnland
    assembly, 68, 69
    laws, 80
    utopian, 68
Houyhnhnms
    astronomy, knowledge of, 69
    breed for strength and comeliness, 68
    burial of dead, 69
    described idyllically, 57
    diet, 58
    Gulliver compared to, 81
    Gulliver identifies with, 78
    innocence of, 61, 80
    language, 60
    lying, ignorance of, 60, 62, 80
    marriage, 68
    "perfection of nature", 60, 61, 93
    poetry, 69
    reason, embodiment of, 80
    Yahoos compared, 58, 62, 81, 87
human nature
    Brobdingnagian king's opinion of, 37
    Gulliver's Travels as commentary on, 83, 86, 93
    ideal of the mean, 89
    reason, 87
    virtue, capable of, 88

I

"I cannot but conclude ... your natives to be the most pernicious race" quote, 37, 89, 94
ideal of the mean, 89
IDG Books Web sites, 96
Imagining Monsters (Todd), 96
immortality, 54
insect imagery, 37
Ireland
    coinage debasement, 44, 46
    England, relation to, 3, 45
    Swift's defense of, 3, 44, 83
Ireland, Church of. See Church of Ireland, Swift's career with

J

Jacobites, 22, 23, 25, 79
Jaffe, Lee, 97
James II, 18
Japan, 55
Japanese, the, 55
Johnson, Esther, 3
Jonathan Swift Page, The, Web site, 97
Jonathan Swift: A Portrait, (Glendinning), 96
Journal to Stella, The (Swift), 3
Juvenal, 44

K

Kendal, Duchess of, 16
Kilkenny Grammar School, 2

L

Lagado, 47
language
    Adam and Eve, 60
    Balnibarbians, 48
    Dutch, 60
    Houyhnhnms, 60
    Sprat's proposal to Royal Society, 48
    technical language, mockery of, 45
Laputa, 43
Laputan king
    Balnibarbi, tyranny over, 45
    Gulliver, hospitality to, 44
    introduced, 8

Laputans
  abstractions, preoccupation with, 86
  clothing, 43
  as philosophers, 44
  wives, whoring, 43, 44
Laud, Archbishop, 18
law
  Brobdingnag, 38, 39
  England, 64, 79
  Houyhnhnland, 80
  Lilliput, 19, 21, 79
legal profession, 62, 64
Lemuel Gulliver. See Gulliver
lice, giant, 33
Lilliput
  Blefuscu, war with, 17
  customs, 21
  education system, 21
  egg-breaking question, 17
  as England, 16, 40, 77, 78, 83
  High Heel party, 8, 17, 18
  Imperial Council, 13
  laws, 19, 21, 79
  Low Heel party, 8, 17, 18
  political office gained by rope
    dancing, 15
  religion, 17
  rulers, pettiness of, 16, 18, 93
  semi-Utopian society, 21
  threads, rewards of, 15
Lilliput, Emperor of
  described, 13
  George I, resemblance to, 13
  Gulliver, grants Nardac title to, 19
  Gulliver, pact with, 15
  Gulliver, plots to starve, 23
  introduced, 7
Lilliput, Empress of, 19
Lilliputians
  Brobdingnagians compared, 27
  character, 78
  children, 89
  cruelty of, 23, 77
  doll-like, 13
  marriage, 21
  pretensions, 17
Lindalino, 45, 46
Little Endians, 18
Locke, John, 85
Lorbrulgrud, 29
Low Heel party, 8, 17, 18
Luggnagg, 53
Lustrog, 17

Luther, Martin, 43
lying, 36, 51, 62, 77, 80

M

Mandeville, Bernard, 65
marriage, 21, 65, 68
Martian moons, Swift's description of, 45
Martinus Scriblerus Club, 5
Marvels of Swift, The, Web site, 97
Master, The. *See* Grey Horse
mathematics, 43
Mechanical Operation of the Spirit, The
    (Swift), 3
Mendez, Pedro de, 73, 87, 88
Mildendo, 17
mirror, Gulliver unable to look into, 40
Moderns, 3, 39, 51, 84, 90
Modest Proposal, A (Swift), 3
modesty, 34, 60, 80. *See also* clothing;
    nakedness
money, 65
moral virtue
  of Brobdingnagians, 28, 29, 77, 79, 84
  God central to, 85
  of Gulliver, 11, 25, 77
  of politicians, 25
  size denoting, 33, 77, 84, 94
  of Swift, 90
More, Thomas, 22, 68
Munodi, 47
music, 43, 44, 47

N

nakedness, 34, 60. *See also* clothing
Nardac title given to Gulliver, 19
Newton, Isaac, 44

O

*Oxford Illustrated History of the British
    Monarchy, The* (Cannon and Griffiths),
    96
Oxford University, 2

P

palace fire, 19, 23
paradox, Swift's use of, 64
"pernicious race of little odious vermin"
    quote, 37, 89, 94

philosophers, 51
Plato, 22, 68
Pleasures of the Imagination (Brewer), 96
Pope, Alexander, 85
pretense, 17
pride. *See also* Gulliver: pride
    in reason, 43, 84, 85
    vice, mixed with, 78

Q

Queen Anne, 20, 83

R

Ramus, Petrus, 51
rationalism, 84, 85
reason. *See also* Deism; science
    animalism versus, 78
    exaltation of, 86
    Houyhnhnm, 80, 86
    immorality, relation to, 44
    love of, 85
    Luther on, 43
    pride in, 43, 84, 85
    Swift's opinion of, 43
    untrustworthy, 50, 54
    vice excused by, 64
    will versus, 85
Redriff, 55
Reldresal, 15–17, 78
religion
    satire, 17, 19, 23
    wars of, 17, 19
Republic (Plato), 22
rich, the, 65
rope dancing, 15
Royal Society, 45, 48

S

science, 43, 47, 48. *See also* reason
Scotus, 51
Shorter, Catherine, 22, 44
Sinon, 75
Skyresh Bolgolam, 19, 23
Slamecksan. *See* Low Heel party
Sprat, Thomas, 48
St. Patrick's Cathedral (Dublin), 2
"Still to Seek: Politics, Irony, Swift"
    (Richardson), 98

Struldbruggs, 54
style of writing
    language, coarse, 20, 88
    matter-of-fact tone, 17, 56
    mock seriousness, 89
    notes, use of, 50
    paradox, 64
    prosaic, 56
    puns, 89
    satiric tone, 88
    scientific papers, parody of, 45
    understatement, 89
sunshine from cucumbers experiment, 48
Swift, Jonathan
    childhood, 2
    church career, 2, 20, 36, 83
    death, 3
    declared incompetent, 3
    defender of Ireland, 3, 44
    education, 2
    Gulliver contrasted with, 90–92, 94
    literary career, 3
    as misanthrope, 87, 89, 94
    moral virtue of, 90
    satirist, 88–90
    science, thoughts on, 90
    Whigs, contempt for, 83

T

Tale of a Tub (Swift), 3, 19
Temple, William, Sir, 2, 83
Test Act, 3
Thistle, Order of the, 15
Tories, 18, 19, 23, 83
Townshend, Viscount, 16, 78
Tramecksan. *See* High Heel party
travel literature genre, 5
treason
    Bishop Atterbury affair, 22, 49
    discerned by reading excrement, 49
    Gulliver accused of, 23
    Harley/Bolingbroke affair, 13, 23, 25
    Lilliputian law concerning, 21
Trinity College, 2

U

Utopia (More), 22
Utrecht, Treaty of, 16, 19, 83

V

venereal diseases, 51, 65
vice
    diet symbolizing, 65
    Gulliver's Travels as critique of, 5
    private versus public, 65
    reason, excused by, 64
    taxation of, 49
    virtue presented as, 89
Virgil, 75
virtue. *See* moral virtue
voyage literature genre, 5

W

Walpole, Robert
    election rigging, 36
    Flimnap as, 15, 78
    resignation, 16
    war, views on, 16
    wife's alleged misconduct, 22, 44
War of the Spanish Succession, 19
Westminster Hall, 11
"When I thought of my family" quote, 72,
    94
Whigs
    church appointments, 36
    Harley/Bolingbroke treason accusations,
        13, 19
    Low Heel party, characterized by, 18
    pettiness of, 16
    Swift's contempt for, 83
    Treaty of Utrecht invalidity claim, 16, 83
    vote buying, 36
    war, conduct of, 19, 41
will versus reason, 85
"Windsor Prophecy, The" (Swift), 3
Wood, William, 46

Y

Yahoos
    as animals, 81
    beasts of burden, 69
    body parts, Gulliver uses, 71
    character, 81
    described, 57, 81
    diet, 58
    English Yahoos, 75, 78
    European Yahoos, 62, 67
    excrement, association with, 87
    extermination of, 69
    Gulliver as, 70, 74
    Gulliver compared to, 81
    Gulliver, defecate on, 56, 57
    Gulliver sees humanity as, 72, 73, 87
    Gulliver separates himself from, 78
    Houyhnhnms compared, 58, 62, 81, 87
    human, recognizing as, 57
    humans, genetic relation to, 67